Narrative and Ideology

Open Guides to Literature

Series Editor: Graham Martin (Professor of Literature, The Open University)

Titles in the Series

Narrative and Ideology

Open Guides to Literature

Series Editor: Graham Martin (Professor of Literature, The Open University)

Titles in the Series

JEREMY TAMBLING

Narrative and Ideology

Open University Press
Milton Keynes · *Philadelphia*

Open University Press
Celtic Court
22 Ballmoor
Buckingham
MK18 1XW

and
1900 Frost Road, Suite 101
Bristol, PA 19007, USA

First Published 1991

British Library Cataloguing-in-Publication Data

Tambling, Jeremy
 Narrative and ideology. – (Open guides to
 literature)
 I. Title   II. Series
 808.3

 ISBN 0-335-09355-8
 ISBN 0-335-09354-X pbk

Library of Congress Cataloging-in-Publication Data

Tambling, Jeremy.
 Narrative and ideology/Jeremy Tambling.
  p.   cm.
 Includes bibliographical references and index.
  ISBN 0-335-09355-8.   ISBN 0-335-09354-X (pbk.)
  1. Narration (Rhetoric)   2. Ideology and literature.   I. Title.
 PN212.T3   1991
 809'.923—dc20   91-23555
                                                   CIP

Typeset by Best-set Typesetter Ltd.
Printed in Great Britain by J.W. Arrowsmith Ltd., Bristol

Contents

In memory of my mother,
Elizabeth Edith Tambling
1913–1991

Series Editor's Preface

The intention of this series is to provide short introductory books about major writers, texts, and literary concepts for students of courses in Higher Education which substantially or wholly involve the study of Literature.

The series adopts a pedagogic approach and style similar to that of Open University material for Literature courses. *Open Guides* aim to inculcate the reading 'skills' which many introductory books in the field tend, mistakenly, to assume that the reader already possesses. They are, in this sense, 'teacherly' texts, planned and written in a manner which will develop in the reader the confidence to undertake further independent study of the topic. They are 'open' in two senses. First, they offer a three-way tutorial exchange between the writer of the *Guide*, the text or texts in question, and the reader. They invite readers to join in an exploratory discussion of texts, concentrating on their key aspects and on the main problems which readers, coming to the texts for the first time, are likely to encounter. The flow of a *Guide* 'discourse' is established by putting questions for the reader to follow up in a tentative and searching spirit, guided by the writer's comments, but not dominated by an over-arching and single-mindedly-pursued argument or evaluation, which itself requires to be 'read'.

Guides are also 'open' in a second sense. They assume that literary texts are 'plural', that there is no end to interpretation, and that it is for the reader to undertake the pleasurable task of discovering meaning and value in such texts. *Guides* seek to provide, in compact form, such relevant biographical, historical and cultural information as bears upon the reading of the text, and they point the reader to a selection of the best available critical discussions of it. They are not in themselves concerned to propose, or to counter, particular readings of the texts, but rather to put *Guide* readers in a position to do that for themselves. Experienced travellers learn to dispense with guides, and so it should be for readers of this series.

This *Open Guide* to *Narrative and Ideology* is best studied in conjunction with *The Penguin Book of English Short Stories* for 'Fanny and Annie' and with *Labyrinths* for 'The Garden of Forking Paths'.

Graham Martin

Introduction

Those readers used to studying popular culture, or media or film studies, will be very familiar with the importance of the word 'narrative' in my title; but people with a more conventional literature background, for whom one of the problems of studying books is remembering the plot, and thinking that it is generally a nuisance, may be more puzzled. This book tries to see why it matters that texts exist in the form of stories: the word 'ideology' appears in the title in order to suggest that the stories we can tell rest on cultural, social assumptions that we may well be unaware of.

Like my earlier book in this series, *What is Literary Language?* this study owes much to literature summer school teaching for the Open University; but it also derives from teaching for the OU Popular Culture course, one of its most adventurous and exciting courses of the eighties. For to look at popular culture is to realize how the media, film, television and fiction, or investigative journalism, or documentaries all cast experience in narrative forms. We cannot escape life being presented to us in a series of 'stories'.

My colleagues Ackbar Abbas and Jonathan Hall have given much help with the writing of this, especially in their detailed comments on the first draft. I would also like to acknowledge Jonathan Hall for his translation of 'Borges and I' and discussions thereon and to Alianza Editorial, Madrid. Graham Martin as the series editor has throughout been encouraging and thought-provoking in his criticisms, making me refine what I wanted to say. My wife Pauline has taken time out from her own work in order to help me in this.

1. Narrative and Ideology

> Myself will straight aboad and to the state
> This heavy act with heavy heart relate.

These are the last lines of Shakespeare's *Othello*. The hero, his wife Desdemona and her servant Emilia are dead on stage; another death (Roderigo's), has taken place off-stage. Having watched the play, we hear Lodovico, a noble Venetian, who has arrived in Cyprus too late to avert the tragedy, say that he will return to Venice to tell the state of Venice the story we have witnessed. The play completes a circle. To tell the story adequately would mean performing *Othello* again.

This study will return to *Othello*, itself a play about telling stories. Othello has won his wife, Desdemona, by telling her the story of his life. Telling stories can be used for erotic effect. Iago spends his time making up stories on the spur of the moment to deceive Roderigo and Othello. Othello's last big speech, before he kills himself, is the demand that people tell the correct story about himself – 'Speak of me as I am' (v. ii. 338). Othello's appeal for a truthful narrative about himself is countered by his desire to project a flattering image, as when he describes himself as 'one that loved not wisely but too well', which may be an example of him cheering himself up (so T.S. Eliot). To persuade, to deceive, to cast the truth in the light most favourable to the narrator – these seem to be some of the functions of telling a story, giving what Othello calls 'a round [i.e. blunt] unvarnished tale' (i. iii. 90).

But it seems from *Othello* that no tale can be round and unvarnished. Stories may convey information, but they also convey much more besides, and in the case of some of those told in the play, much less. So why is story-telling so popular? How many different types of story are we exposed to during the course of a week? How many kinds of narrative can you think of? Newspaper headlines, television plays – can you continue the list?

DISCUSSION

I give two answers: my own and that of Roland Barthes (1915–80), the French critic who pioneered work on narrative in the 1960s. I have cut out from my list places of overlap with his:

Advertisements; directions for use on washing powder packets; instructions how to enter a competition sent to you in the post with your personal name added from the computer files; comic strips; novels; poems; short stories in magazines; plays; operas; folk-song; programme music (such as Berlioz's *Symphonie Fantastique*); overtures (e.g. *William Tell*); holiday brochures (taking you through the day – telling you what you can do from morning to night); personal or official letters; complaints, in whatever form these are made; TV interviews of politicians, or *Desert Island Discs*; peep shows; ceremonies, such as weddings or Remembrance Day, which record events either happening, or that have happened; accounts of the self made to the police, to a priest, a doctor, a teacher, at a job interview; sermons; jokes; birth, marriage and death certificates; old tombstones.

Barthes:

> The narratives of the world are numberless. Able to be carried by articulated language, spoken or written, fixed or moving images, gestures and the ordered mixture of all these substances; narrative is present in myth, legend, fable, tale, novella, epic, history, tragedy, drama, comedy, mime, painting (think of Carpaccio's *Saint Ursula*), stained glass windows, cinema, comics, news items, conversation. Moreover... narrative is present in every age, in every place, in every society; it begins with the very history of mankind, and there nowhere is nor has been a people without narrative.[1]

Your reaction to these lists may be: 'Well, I suppose many of these examples – like sermons – do include telling stories in them, but they involve much more than that – the story is not all there is.' (This is also true of many novels.) Later on I shall want to return to this, suggesting that each of these forms not only *contains*, but *is* narrative. But at present, it is enough to agree about the multiplicity of stories and types of stories there are that surround us.

But if directions on a packet constitute a story or narrative, what do we mean by narrative? In a sense the whole of this *Guide* examines this question. But provisionally, the point may be put like this: when we think of how to use a detergent, there is immediately set up in our minds a before and after – a sequence of events. One brand name I checked had 'Before use' and 'After use' written on the box. This 'A followed by B' sequence gives the base of a narrative. And thinking about how to use a soap powder can

only be done in narrative – sequential – terms: as though humans have to make up stories to do anything.

Immediately we start thinking about types of narrative and types of story-telling, we realize that 'literature' – plays, poems, novels – provides only a small selection of types. Present-day ('postmodern') reality is to be surrounded by narrative voices:

> Captured by the radio (the voice is the law) as soon as he awakens, the listener walks all day long through the forest of narrativities from journalism, advertising and television, narrativities that still find time, as he is getting ready for bed, to slip a few final messages under the portals of sleep...these stories have a providential and predestinating function: they organize in advance our work, our celebrations and even our dreams....[2]

The questions de Certeau raises are, then, who tells these influential stories, how do they get into circulation, and what conscious and unconscious influences do they have? To think of a society that tells itself stories in accordance with its cherished ways of seeing and believing is to ask about the relationship of narratives to ideology. 'Postmodernism' (of which more in the last chapter) believes that social existence has been taken over by controlling narratives that focalize our ways of seeing. As de Certeau puts it, punning on the French word *récit* (story), 'our society has become a recited society in three senses: it is defined by stories (*récits*, the fables constituted by our advertising and informational media), by *citations* of stories, and by the interminable *recitations* of stories' (p. 186). To investigate narratives means investigating the everyday life beliefs that operate through a culture.

In this study it is specialized types of narratives, in novels and drama and poems, that we shall mainly be thinking of. But it seems that literature is and gives just a select set of ways of telling a story. Barthes implies that there is a narrative structure involved in almost everything we are involved in: narrative 'is simply there, like life itself'.

But we could never be influenced consciously or unconsciously by narratives if it were not for the fascination of the story and story-telling. In *Aspects of the Novel*, E.M. Forster (1879–1970) asserts that 'the fundamental aspect of the novel is its story-telling aspect'. He goes on to break that down by imagining the responses of three sets of people to the question, 'What does a novel do?' The first, a bus-driver, says no more than 'I suppose it kind of tells a story so to speak'; the second and third give more detail – that which a novelist would give: these people sound like characters from Forster's own fictions:

Another man, whom I visualize as on a golf-course, will be aggress-
ive and brisk. He will reply: 'What does a novel do? Why, tell a
story of course, and I've no use for it if it didn't. I like a story. You
can take your art, you can take your literature, you can take your
music, but give me a good story. And I like a story to be a story,
mind, and my wife's the same.' And a third man, he says in a sort
of drooping regretful voice, 'Yes – oh dear yes – the novel tells a
story.' I respect and admire the first speaker, I detest and fear the
second. And the third is myself.[3]

This caricatures people's attitudes – the homely working-class
type, the club-swinging Surrey stockbroker, and the hesitant,
decent, liberal novelist – but the elements of overstatement
perhaps should not allow us to think we know any better than
critics in the 1920s why the idea of a story should be so important
to literature.

Why do people read novels? The golf-player type would
answer, according to E.M. Forster, that we read/watch television
drama/get the news ('Now over to our reporter in Washington for
tonight's main story...' – you hear something like this almost
every evening on television news) for the 'story'. There may be a
number of other reasons, too, but this is an obvious one. But till
the late eighteenth century, when novel reading became established, most people, though no doubt like Saint Paul's Athenians,
'spending their time in nothing else but either to tell or to hear
some new thing' (Acts 17:21) knew the stories of the literature
they read or saw. Neither Sophocles (496–406 BC) nor Shakespeare
told original stories. Knowing the story does not necessarily put
people off reading or re-reading: some people like to read the end
of a novel before the beginning. The originality of the story is not
in itself enough to account for its appeal.

Nor, indeed, would a summary of the story that Lodovico
might tell the Venetian senate indicate the fascination of the play:
'Iago, Othello's Ancient, angry that he had been passed over for
promotion in favour of Cassio, persuaded Othello straight after he
had married Desdemona that his wife had committed adultery
with Cassio. He also involved Roderigo, who was in love with
Desdemona, and wanted to possess her, in his plot. Othello killed
Desdemona, believing her to be false, and killed himself when he
learned his mistake. Iago, who killed his wife Emilia when she
realized the truth, survives to be tortured.' When I read summaries
like this, my eyes glaze over and I lose concentration: if I know the
text well, I want to pick holes in the summary.

As they say about jokes, it all depends on how you tell them.
What other ingredients are there involved in telling a story? E.M.
Forster distinguishes *story* and *plot*:

> We have defined a story as a narrative of events arranged in their
> time sequence. A plot is also a narrative of events, the emphasis
> falling on causality. 'The king died and then the queen died' is a
> story. 'The king died and then the queen died of grief' is a plot. The
> time-sequence is preserved, but the sense of causality overshadows
> it. Or again, 'The queen died, no one knew why, until it was
> discovered it was through grief at the death of the king.' This is a
> plot with a mystery in it, a form capable of high development. It
> suspends the time-sequence, it moves as far away from the story as
> its limitations will allow. Consider the death of the queen. If it is in
> a story we say, 'and then?' If it is in a plot we ask 'why?' ... A plot
> demands intelligence and memory [as well as curiosity, essential for
> the story].
>
> *(Aspects of the Novel*, pp. 93–4)

Forster's concept of plot makes a tale no longer 'round and
unvarnished'. My account of the story of *Othello* left out such
questions as why Iago wants to take such a full revenge, and
why a revenge of this type; why Othello believes him and not
Desdemona; why Othello is so insanely angry with Desdemona;
why Emilia is so compliant to Iago till the end. Each of these
questions raises critical problems: none can be answered simply at
the 'story' level; it might be said that the play exists, indeed, to
provoke such questions.

That said, **do you agree with Forster's distinction between
'story' and 'plot'? It may be useful to begin by rephrasing it, in
your own words. What does the 'story' bring into prominence?
What does the 'plot' foreground? In what ways is the distinction
'story'/'plot' useful?**

DISCUSSION

I think the distinction helps in that it emphasizes a difference that
needs to be made in at least some cases: between the *narrative* (i.e.
the 'story') and the way it has been *narrativized* (turned into
narrative). 'Story' and 'plot' give the same narrative of the king
and queen, but the plot acts as a way of narrativizing the events,
of giving them body and substance.

Returning to an earlier point: not till the eighteenth-century
novel did stories become compulsorily 'novel', original, new. Until
then, narrations were often basically variations on themes. Take
some examples: how many variants of the Cinderella narrative are
there? The rags-to-riches theme at the heart of the Cinderella story
is the basis of many Mills and Boon romances, for instance. The
narratives of King Arthur have been plotted in numerous ways:
think of Malory, Tennyson, T.H. White, Lerner and Loewe in
Camelot – as well as the numerous medieval romance redactions

of the basic narrative. It may be possible to construct a single life of Jesus from the four Gospels – though to harmonize the way Matthew, Mark, Luke and John record events is difficult or impossible – but actually what exists in the New Testament is four separate narratives of Jesus, all purporting to plot the same story. Many jokes are simply variants on the same story line, usually with the characters updated. The distinction is worth preserving, though I prefer to use the terms 'narrative' and 'narrativizing' to make it, since 'story' and 'plot' are open to strong objections which need discussing.

Forster sees the story as causally linked to time – events happen as A then B then C. On Forster's basis, a society without a sense of time's passing could not tell a story. A plot is well aware of the existence of time, but keeps it in the background; instead it stresses that events in time are linked as cause and effect – B happens because A brings it about, and the consequence is C. A plot is more interested in the value of events than simply the fact that they occur, and the value of an event includes its cause or origin (why it happened), and its afterlife, its power to produce further events. A plot thus reveals that events have significance: just because something happens (the story) does not make it important, any more than being five minutes in the company of one person is the same as being five minutes in the company of someone else.

Hence Forster demotes the story's importance in that first quotation given from *Aspects of the Novel*. But I have two objections to this. First, he assumes a world of causality, where it is demonstrable that A produces B, and so on, in a chain of cause and effect. This fits some forms of Realist and Naturalist fiction where the writer (e.g. Zola, or George Eliot) wants to prove that there is a 'scientific' link between events. Eliot is often accused of determinism, owing to her desire to show that characters cannot change their destinies because of their past existences. Mr Bulstrode, the fraudulent banker in *Middlemarch* (1872) is an example of this: 'The train of causes in which he had locked himself went on' (Ch. 61, Penguin edn. (1965) p. 665). Forster's fiction uses the same presuppositions. But the distinction hardly fits Modernist writing, which attacks such ideas as causality as so much nineteenth-century ideology.

For instance, Kafka's short story *Metamorphosis* (published in 1915) begins: 'As Gregor Samsa awoke one morning from uneasy dreams he found himself transformed in his bed into a gigantic insect'. Clearly, 'causality' means nothing in the context of such writing; nothing *causes* Gregor Samsa to become an insect,

though once it has happened, Kafka plays wittily with all the things that respectable parents would do when they discovered that such a scandal had taken place in their own house. Similarly, in Beckett's *Waiting for Godot*, think of the way that the play refuses the idea that any one event is linked to any other event. In the second act, one tramp (Vladimir), remembers that he and the other were together in the first act; the other (Estragon), has no memory of this. Perhaps the same point applies to Shakespeare. One difficulty in understanding *Othello* may be that we expect it to have a 'rational' A causes B pattern to it: it is not clear that the play is not more episodic than that (i.e. story, not plot), and that the drama of the early Modern period questions such nineteenth-century novel-like linkings up and 'realistic' consistencies.

This leads in to my second objection, which is a more difficult point. Forster seems committed to a conventional understanding of what a story and plot are; he does not question that there must be a sequence of events in what is written. The conventionality appears in the doubtless unconscious choice of subject given in the example: a king and queen, as though these were the important types of people to write about! (His fictional practice is better than that, I should add.) Doesn't the concept of causality set the agenda for writing about subjects with clearly defined edges, where events can be delineated as such? Feminist criticism, which emphasizes how male-oriented History writing is (History is the history that men experience) makes a significant intervention in emphasizing that events are not naturally describable as such: they are so designated because of the weight of ideological pressure. Thus Virginia Woolf, whose *A Room of One's Own* (1929) virtually inaugurates feminist criticism of the novel, and at least implicitly takes issue with Forster:

> And since a novel has this correspondence to real life, its values are to some extent those of real life. But it is obvious that the values of women differ very often from the values which have been made by the other sex; naturally this is so. Yet it is the masculine values that prevail. Speaking crudely, football and sport are 'important'; the worship of fashion, the buying of clothes 'trivial'. And these values are inevitably transferred from life to fiction. This is an important book, the critic assumes, because it deals with war. This is an insignificant book because it deals with the feelings of women in a drawing-room. A scene in a battlefield is more important than a scene in a shop – everywhere and much more subtly the difference of value persists.

Elsewhere, Woolf envisages a fiction having 'no plot, no comedy, no tragedy, no love interest or catastrophe in the accepted style'.[4]

She wishes to cut away at the assumptions Forster makes about the proper stuff of narrative, implicit in his story/plot distinctions which assume certain definite actions making up a narrative. Action in a Woolf novel seems much more difficult to pin down, much less involved in 'masculine values' which seem so much the feature of realist texts. The ways in which different values permeate narratives reflect ideological considerations; the dominant views of a society means that a society gets the narratives its ideological presuppositions support. (Later, the word 'reflect' may seem inadequate to describe the relationship between narrative and ideology.)

Aspects of Narrative

A narrative, then, includes a story and a plot, and is much more than these things. The term 'narrative' seems preferable to 'story', because it makes no value-laden assumptions that some events are trivial (like gossip) or important (ready to be turned into a novel or made part of history); nor does it assume that events have causal relationships between each other which can be easily plotted and known in an objective manner. 'Plot', though it goes beyond the concept of the unstructured and episodic 'story', and may prompt thought as to how episodes can be linked causally, is also a heavily ideological term, assuming the validity of explanation, and thus I find it less useful than the word 'narrative'.

When we read, though we have not yet answered the question why people find a story attractive, it needs to be said that we are brought under the lure of narrative. And in a text there are several possible narratives at work.

Let me illustrate these two points with an example: the opening of Milton's *Paradise Lost* (1674), an epic in twelve books, giving the history of Genesis (Chapters 1–3 – the fall of Adam and Eve) with added lessons for Milton's contemporary audience. The extract invokes the Holy Spirit, asking for inspiration, as classical writers began with an *invocatio* to the Muse. What makes this passage, which is not telling a story, or giving a plot, actually a narrative? What possible stories are generated here?

> Of Man's First Disobedience and the Fruit
> Of that Forbidden Tree, whose mortal tast [taste]
> Brought Death into the World, and all our wöe,
> With loss of Eden, till one greater Man
> Restore us, and regain the blissful Seat,
> Sing Heav'nly Muse, that on the secret top
> Of Oreb or of Sinai, didst inspire

> That Shepherd, who first taught the chosen Seed
> In the Beginning how the Heav'ns and Earth
> Rose out of Chaos: or if Sion Hill
> Delight thee more, and Siloa's Brook that flow'd
> Fast by the Oracle of God; I thence
> Invoke thy aid to my adventrous Song,
> That with no middle flight intends to soar
> Above th' Aonian Mount, while it pursues
> Things unattempted yet in Prose or Rhime.

('That forbidden tree' – God prohibited Adam and Eve from eating of the Tree of Knowledge of Good and Evil, an edict they disobeyed. The 'Shepherd' is Moses, who wrote Genesis, given to him by inspiration on Mount Horeb or Sinai; 'the chosen seed' are the Israelites. Sion refers to Jersualem; Siloa is the name of a stream near the Temple, here called 'the oracle of God'. The Aonian Mount is Helicon, the hill sacred to the classical Greek Muses.)

DISCUSSION

As a prelude written according to epic conventions (those of Homer and Virgil), clearly this extract itself is not telling the story of *Paradise Lost*. Yet to say just that is too simple. For the first five lines do give the Biblical story in miniature; and it should be noticed that Milton assumes in those lines that his readers know the story ('that forbidden tree', for instance, relies on its effect on nobody saying, 'Which one do you mean?'. Similarly with 'that Shepherd'. These are instances of a *cultural code* Milton is using – we will return to this topic). There is no wish to tell something original (though you may feel that the last line contradicts this point). 'Knowing the story' is much more than just being familiar with a particular account, it implies accepting the cultural presuppositions involved in the Biblical narration: these are held as part of the religious and political ideology of the period, though struggle raged in the seventeenth century over interpretations of the Bible.

Though Milton is not writing a plot, it is clear that he believes in causality, in blame and guilt, in the fact that Eden was lost for a reason. Five consequences of the 'mortal taste' of the fruit Adam and Eve ate from are revealed; so he is ready to think in terms of plot, in Forster's sense.

Further, while not offering a story, the writing follows a sequence which is that of the Old Testament. The first geographical references are to Eden; the second are to the wilderness and to the exodus of the Israelites from Egypt; the third is to Jerusalem and the temple, founded when the Israelites were settled in the land. Thus there is a narrative here: Milton does not think outside the pattern of Old Testament history in its linear shape.

But to call this a narrative is to draw attention to other points:

1 That the writer has put this material into a particular form, has thought of this particular way to present it.
2 That the text is intended to impart textual information (other possible narratives), quite apart from being an invocation.
3 That the text is intended to give a sense (itself a narrative) of the voice speaking this: to create the impression of the author as prophet.

Can you comment on possible reasons for any of these three reasons? With regard to the first, can you see a consistent or changing attitude to the epic style? If there is change, is a narrative created out of that? For the second point, can you see any other narratives at work? For the third, in what ways does the narrator characterize himself?

DISCUSSION

1 Even if you know little of the classical epic's invocation of the Muse, you will see how the writing changes shape: the Holy Spirit is referred to in line 6, and it is assumed that it will be the narrator. By the end of the extract, the narrator's confidence is up: it is 'my adventrous song', which is going to transcend the poetry of the heathen epic. There is a criticism of the classical form, and a sense of daring. He has begun with 'disobedience', which implies a crossing of limits, but it is clear that he himself intends to respect no limits: there seems to be a narrative of change here as well as a commitment to his own narrative.
2 There is much information here which points to other narratives. The Shepherd is glossed as the one who 'first taught the chosen Seed/In the Beginning how the Heav'ns and Earth/Rose out of Chaos'. Moses taught the Israelites about the beginning of the world: note that a spiritual leader is said to be a narrator, a story-teller. Milton intends a comparison between himself and Moses, and between Israel and the English in the seventeenth century. The reference to the 'oracle of God' invites comparison with the Greek oracle at Delphi. 'Soar' may well suggest the eagle, itself a traditional emblem of inspiration and fabled to be able to look steadily at the sun: perhaps Milton compares his song and its

insights with his own blind condition. If so, this reference aligns himself with Homer, also supposed to have been blind, and so begins to set up another narrative, one conveying a sense of the narrator.

3 Definitions that might apply to the narrator are (a) that he appears to be humble, (b) supremely confident, (c) assured of the value of the material being used, and (d) writing material more than epic in scope. The reader is to gather that the authority of the 'Heav'nly Muse', of Moses, of 'the Oracle of God' (both the name of a place and the description of God's sayings) is at work here, teaching and instructing – both words used in the text. Milton the seventeenth-century writer is swallowed up in this authoritative narrator, who is a projection of the poet – his narrative of himself – constructing himself as a writer who by another narrative fictionalizing is not the actual writer, but simply the secretary of the Muse – though we have agreed that there is a contradiction here. What is crucial is that the narrator is not an identical concept to that of the author. In discussing these narratives in the text, which nonetheless is not principally giving a narrative, but introducing the poem, we can see that there is an elaborate crisscrossing involved, whereby one point in the text suggests several narrative links, or codes, or concatenations of significances. To investigate a text as complex as this one of Milton's, which does not stop (note that it is all one sentence: 'soaring' and 'pursuing' in earnest), which weaves one narrative set of expectations with another, means beginning with the proposition that it is worth seeing any text in terms of a narrative, as generating narratives and using ones already written.

To isolate how those links or codes are articulated in the text ('articulated' meaning both 'spoken' and 'joined together', as an articulated truck is connected up) I want to go on to discuss a short story by D.H. Lawrence (1885–1930), 'Fanny and Annie'.[5] If you have not read this before, it should take you about 20 minutes to do it; the next chapter will assume that you can work upon it from the basis of at least one reading.

2. 'Fanny and Annie'

Taking 'Fanny and Annie' as narrative – so registering that it is crafted in specific ways – means finding traditional tools of criticism both helpful and obscuring. Reading as narrative means not assuming that it is simply a work of art, cleverly or not cleverly done, depending on your point of view. The traditional terms concede too much to the author and to the form in which the text comes. To take it as a narrative means considering it as an act of communication, with definite designs and with methods of making sure it tells the best story – the best from the point of view of the sender of the message.

What are these traditional terms of criticism? I want to look at them altogether in this chapter, before going on to consider them individually later on. We may begin with Aristotle's sense of the different elements at work in writing. Aristotle (384–322 BC) in the *Poetics* (*c.*330 BC), a source-book for much western literary criticism, discussed primarily tragedy and epic, which he considered differed from dramatic tragedy, being 'in narrative form'.[1] The presence of plot and character were basic to both. Thus picking up on Aristotle's definitions, take these elements for 'Fanny and Annie':

1   the narrative form which requires a narrator and reader/ hearer;
2   the plot – the 'representation of the action' – the action as the story, the plot as the organization of this pre-existent material (as we saw when discussing E.M. Forster);
3   the characters.

Later, Aristotle makes further distinctions when (Ch. 23) he discusses time, the duration and presentation of events, and sees that when telling a history, it may well be impossible to keep the narration to chronological time. Earlier (Ch. 5), he had taken a very purist view of the matter and suggested that in tragedy, the time of presentation accorded exactly – or nearly – to the time that the actual events described would take.

We shall return to each of Aristotle's terms. But thinking of 'Fanny and Annie', it might help to make preliminary notes about (a) the narrator and the narrative form, (b) on the plot – what is it (a short summary would help), and where is it going, (c) on the characters – does a pattern emerge for the modes of description used?; and (d) on the ways time is used in the short story.

DISCUSSION

What follows are preliminary comments only:

(a) The narrator and the narrative form
There is a narrator who is not one of the characters of the story; the narrator speaks as in 'Let us confess it at once' (pp. 209, 176) as though stepping out of the frame of the events in the text, and filling in details of an earlier time. The narrator supplies plenty of details: Fanny's background at the beginning; he knows people's motivations, as at the end, when Mrs Goodall is 'flattered and assured' (pp. 223, 190). This comes from the narrator, who knows – indeed, in the wealth of information given, he appears to be omniscient, surveying the action and characters from a point of vantage. He knows what goes on simultaneously, upstairs and downstairs at the Goodalls' house (pp. 221–2, 188–9), though he professes to know no more than Fanny does when Mrs Nixon shouts in the street (pp. 212, 179). In that sense, the narration is deceptive: that is not necessarily meant pejoratively.

(b) The plot, and where it is going
My attempt at a summary of this runs:

> Fanny has returned home from being a lady's maid, and is resigned to marrying her first love, Harry, a foundry-worker. The discovery of another woman in Harry's life – news broadcast in the chapel at harvest festival time by the woman's mother – seems to influence her more firmly to stay.

In what ways does this summary miss elements of the plot?

DISCUSSION

It makes all the events in the text too certain! We do not really know what effect the revelation of Annie's importance has on Fanny; we see Harry through Fanny's eyes, not through those of the narrator, and so have difficulty interpreting his character and his past (does the dialogue between Harry and his family (pp. 221–2, 188–9) where Fanny is not present, tell us more?), we are

not even certain whether she will marry Harry at the end; we do
not know why the title refers to a woman we never see, but who
nonetheless is aligned with Fanny, down to the very rhyming
name; we do not know why Fanny walks back with Harry –
'some obstinacy' (pp. 221, 188) hardly explains anything. In other
words, in terms of causality, the text is thin.

(c) The characters

Characterization seems to exist on fairly definable lines: Fanny
defined by her clothes and her class status; Harry defined by his;
Aunt Lizzie, more petit-bourgeois; Mrs Goodall's 'one vixen of a
married daughter' (pp. 213, 180); Mr Goodall, 'a silent, evasive
sort of man' (pp. 223, 190); Mr Enderby, 'a little simple, one of
God's fools, perhaps, an odd bachelor soul, emotional, ugly, but
very gentle' (pp. 218, 185). There are few surprises here – people
are set up by the narrator in predictable patterns, which may
suggest his attitudes.

(d) The narrative time

Several time-scales appear. Fanny's past twelve years are given in a
single paragraph (pp. 209, 176). A walk of a mile in silence, when
Fanny and Harry might be assumed to be thinking hard, is given
in two neutral lines (pp. 221, 188). The narrative goes back in
time when it goes from downstairs to upstairs at the Goodalls'
(pp. 221–2, 188–9). Annie's thoughts about Harry, beginning,
'Because there was about him ... ' (pp. 216, 183) to the end of
the paragraph, might well encapsulate thoughts she has had for
the past twelve years. Details of the past keep emerging into the
present. Sometimes the narrative cuts a day (pp. 213, 180), sometimes it seems to go at the very tempo of people talking – e.g. the
discussion in church after the service.

The simple point emerging from this is that the handling of
time is itself dictated by considerations which define an incident's
importance by the printed space given to it in a time pattern. The
narration assumes it knows what the important events are. The
reader goes along with this set of valuations of events, and that
readiness to do so indicates the presence of cultural assumptions.
How we consider the flow of events in time and link events
together in a temporal succession, comes from a set of beliefs and
assumptions about time, about what events are important, about
what things people should spend time and energy on, and what
things can be passed over. Further, the ability of narrative to make
leaps in time assumes that the reader is willing to accept the basic
sameness of people within time – that they do not change.

Having made a start on Aristotle's elements which build up
the story, let us go back to what is perhaps the simplest – the plot,
and to Aristotle's definition of what a plot must comprise. It must
be whole, and

> a whole is that which has a beginning, a middle and an end. A
> beginning is that which does not necessarily come after something
> else, although something else exists or comes about after it. An end,
> on the contrary, is that which naturally follows something else
> either as a necessary or as a usual consequence, and is not itself
> followed by anything. A middle is that which follows something
> else, and is itself followed by something.
>
> (*Classical Literary Criticism*, p. 41)

**On the basis of this, which may remind you of E.M. Forster's
ideas of plot, think about 'Fanny and Annie' in terms of its
beginning, middle and end: its beginning point; its conclusion,
(what is concluded?). What events in it may be defined as the
middle?** Before each 'answer' in the discussion I begin by giving
the comments of Lawrence's most famous critic, F.R. Leavis, for
comparison.[2]

Beginning

> It opens with a well-dressed young woman, 'tall and distinguished'
> getting out of the train at a dismal wayside station in the industrial
> Midlands.
>
> (Leavis, p. 89)

DISCUSSION

This seems accurate; nonetheless the concept of a 'beginning' even
here is difficult. For Fanny has come back having been jilted by
her now deceased cousin, and she remembers the cousin in the
chapel with her, 'young, clever, come down from London where
he was getting on well, learning his Latin and his French and
German so brilliantly' (pp. 215, 182). This is another beginning:
as is the letter to Harry which he has responded to (pp. 214, 181).
Yet another point of beginning is Fanny's previous knowledge of
Annie before she left, and whatever happened between Harry and
Annie seems to be another originating moment. Or if we wanted
to go right back, we could find a beginning with the marriage of
the aunt (pp. 213, 180), a marriage which in its unsatisfactoriness
the Aunt feels Fanny is about to repeat.

Beginning a story is difficult. One summary of Dickens's
Great Expectations I read began by recounting how Compeyson
jilted Miss Havisham. Certainly in terms of the chronological

pattern of the novel, this is a valid place to start. In fact, you could start further back, with Magwitch's childhood (recounted in Chapter 41). A beginning represents a choice of viewpoint, a choice of a perspective: in this case, Fanny's, arriving back to see a community as an enclosed world – a familiar point of entry. But its effect is always to construct the story as analogous to a detective plot: the discovery of past beginnings, of other possible entrances. Beginnings inevitably have this effect.

End

> Fanny, whose 'superiority' Mrs Goodall had disliked, has taken her decision; it is a real and full choice, a self-committal, and as such wins a meeting response from Mrs Goodall. Fanny has always been genuinely attracted by Harry, and without any simplifying or sentimentalizing of the situation, we are made to judge that she has chosen life. The sense in which she has done so it takes the tale to define.
>
> (Leavis, pp. 92–3)

DISCUSSION

This reading depends on seeing the words 'Mother', and 'assured' (pp. 223, 190) as keys: Fanny is in a new relationship with Mrs Goodall. Thus the turning point in the narrative is the question, will she or will she not marry Harry? – a crux unfolded on p. 221 – 'Should she?'

Yet the ending is also puzzlingly downbeat, unresolved. There is no conversation between Fanny and Harry for instance, or any sense of what marriage between them would be like: the reader is left to speculate why Fanny has decided to opt for Harry at the end, especially now that she has a perfectly valid reason for not staying with him. It never has been clear, except possibly on the economic grounds that she needs to be married to him (I have heard it speculated that she returns home to get married because she is pregnant) and it remains a puzzle. This is hardly an ending in Aristotle's sense; it invites speculation going beyond the text.

And Leavis's point could not have the same validity if this were not the end of the story anyway. Supposing what we had read was only the first chapter of a novel. In that case, we would put no emphasis on 'Mother' and 'assured', feeling that it would be likely that the next chapter would upset the relationships again. To be perverse, we do not know what will happen next: we give an important weight to the last few words because we have read enough endings to know that this is where the twist will occur. If we did not know how to read a short story, we could ascribe only a limited significance here. The genre dictates the meaning.

Middle
Leavis emphasises a 'moral struggle' (p. 92) within Fanny to come to terms with her plight, 'the stresses and hesitations of the lady's maid, returning unwillingly to her first love, the unambitious foundry-worker' (p. 93).

DISCUSSION

A middle thus is a means to an end – to the moral conclusion provided by the resolution, which retrospectively justifies the middle. But we could read the whole text, on the other hand, as *all* middle, in the sense that it has no beginning and its end seems to have resolved nothing.

The discussion of beginning–middle–end here assumes that Fanny is at the centre of the text. But it is worth noting that the text has already allowed for the possibility of *not* taking her as the centre. The title brings in the shadowy other woman, referred to but not seen. Except in quotation, Leavis never refers to the figure who is the other half of the text. (It is true, of course, that in any case he is discussing the story only parenthetically.) Drawing attention to the title 'de-centres' Fanny from being its main reference point.

I mean we could interrogate what we mean by the plot of 'Fanny and Annie' in another way. We could ask whether the interesting things that happen in the text *happen* to Fanny, or whether she initiates them. What of Annie? Half the narrative takes place off-stage. We only hear the conversation of the woman (pp. 212, 179). The account of Mrs Nixon (pp. 218, 185) is rendered from twelve-year-old Fanny's knowledge of her. Harry's narrative of his affair with Annie (pp. 220, 187–8) is only his text: no other view on it is given. The last two pages give the Goodall family passing narratives on to each other – it seems mainly for Fanny's benefit, to keep her prepared to marry Harry – the truths of which are never given any validation.

And Fanny's past with her cousin Luther (a name itself setting up a narrative!) is also off-stage: indeed, everything that happens, apart from the interruption in the chapel, seems to have taken place off-stage, before the start. Nothing happens when the narrative of Fanny returning to her home takes place: Lawrence seems here to agree with Virginia Woolf that a story which seeks to convey real life would indeed have in it little plot.

At this point, ask whether you feel the text is in any way making a problem out of the idea of its being a short story, giving a single, recognizable linear plot. Can you can make more of the idea of 'de-centring' Fanny from the heart of the text?

DISCUSSION

Several smallish points occur:

1   It is interesting how much of the text consists in people giving narratives to each other – however short: Mrs Nixon, the Goodall family; Fanny to her aunt, Fanny to herself, Harry to Mr Enderby. In a sense, the narrator's narration is no more than any of these. We are free to think of it as equally relative, equally partial. (These narratives serve to build up a sense of community: Leavis's reading of the text would stress the community as the centre of the tale.)

2   Fanny and Annie have known each other – the text is silent beyond that, but that gap in the text invites a filling, even if only to decide that aspects of the tale (is Annie having a child? What will happen to it?) may suggest limitations in what the novelist could write about. In other words, the text raises issues that it cannot deal with. This would de-centre the narrator from the text, if the point is accepted.

3   When the narrator describes 'the faintest sort of a resemblance' between Harry and Mr Enderby (pp. 220, 187), the male relationships implied there seem to exclude Fanny. Indeed, the text could be read as Fanny learning that she is not at the centre of her own drama – that there are things about Harry she cannot know, one of which is the answer to the question whether he is the father of Annie's baby.

If we considered the text as having more than one centre, we would not be so confident as Leavis that there is a firm line running towards an irresistible conclusion. He reads the text as moving towards a narrative *closure* – not his term, but one taken from the philosopher Jacques Derrida (b. 1930), whose philosophical/critical work attacks its possibility and its desirability, since it shuts off the play of possibility – of plurality – within writing ('textuality'). Derrida, like the psychoanalyst and critic Jacques Lacan (1900–81), with whom his work has several affinities, also discusses 'de-centring' throughout his work. Leavis reads in a linear manner, and as the texture of his comments on the end suggests, treats the story as though it dealt with people in a real-life situation, as though the text were holding up the mirror to truth and requiring us to judge from our knowledge of people and of life. 'We are made to judge that she has chosen life' – the text assesses us as much as Fanny and the others. But at that point it might be wiser to take the text as much more problematic, as belonging to a 'realist', nineteenth-century mode (Leavis significantly, and rightly, I think, connects the tale with George Eliot's writing: she has been classically associated with realism). 'Realism', to define that term in a preliminary way, assumes a textual authority over the characters and incidents, and it purports to say, 'people are like this'.

An Alternative Approach

A post-structuralist approach to narrative theory makes this viewpoint harder to sustain. For it insists on the illusory nature of the real as conveyed in fiction, simply because fiction *is* fictional, not real, and made up of language, whose property is to come already freighted with connotations, with narrative indicators that run through it at both conscious and unconscious levels.

Thus Roland Barthes sees two associative fields, two sets of networks organizing reading at the linear, start-to-finish plot level of narrative. These points link together as codes, which are 'simply associative fields, a supratextual organization of notations which impose a certain idea of structure . . . the codes are certain types of "déjà-lu" [already read], of "déjà-fait" [already done, already experienced]: the code is the form of this "déjà"'. The codes thus insert the reader into a world already known, already defined. The code is 'a corpus of rules that are so worn that we take them to be marks of nature; but if the narrative departed from them, it would very rapidly become unreadable'.[3] The idea of the code being so familiar as to seem natural means that it functions perfectly as ideology, i.e. as part of the unconscious assumptions working in a culture, taken for granted and assumed to be universally valid.

Barthes refers to an 'action code', (the proairetic code) which manifests itself in actions and the decisions necessary to take to do them. Barthes stresses that these actions are always definable in known terms, as 'already-done' or 'already-written' – already codified, known to us through literature which relies upon our ability to see action in these terms.[4] At the same time there is a 'hermeneutic code' which works by posing puzzles, secrets to be unravelled. To quote Barthes, 'To narrate (in the classic [realist – J.T.]) fashion is to raise the question as if it were a subject which one delays predicating; and when the predicate (truth) arrives, the sentence, the narrative, are over' (S/Z, p. 76). In fact, of course, the hermeneutic code constructs the truth it claims to discover: there is no innocent discovery at the end of the text.

What familiar actions construct the plot of 'Fanny and Annie'? What mysteries are set up to await solution? How do these elements structure the onward movement of the narrative as plot?

DISCUSSION

1   The action code. Fanny coming home; the question whether she will marry or not, her revulsion from Harry; her movement towards his family; the incident of the other, Betrayed Woman accusing Harry (I put the point in capitals to emphasize how 'literary' a theme this is), and the drama of the exposure of Harry in the chapel.

2   The hermeneutic code. Most obviously, will Fanny marry Harry? The title poses the question, who is Annie? The woman's intervention (pp. 212, 179) sets up a demand for knowledge – who is she?; later the question of paternity is raised; throughout the text there is revelation of the past, which we have seen to be structural to narratives professing a beginning; and there is the question of what Fanny thinks of Annie, of Harry and Mrs Goodall and her family.

By the end, our questions raised by the hermeneutic code have received a kind of solution, in Leavis's reading; we have been lured by the action code to go on to the end to get the answers, which, by the force of Lawrence's rhetoric, have been made to seem resolutions to profound moral issues.

At the same time Barthes sees codes working vertically along this linear structure of narrative: he sees these codes setting off powerful connotations which intersect with other possibilities of narrative which the reader is familiar with. I will list these codes as they appear in S/Z, and illustrate them in 'Fanny and Annie':

1   The semic or connotative code: this allows the reader to collect thematic features relating to characters in the text and to develop a sense of them as 'characters'. (Go back to what we said about characterization in 'Fanny and Annie', how straightforward it is, and how it depends on the repetition of a few basic phrases about the people.)

2   The symbolic code, which conveys the ideas around which the text is constructed: this, described by Barthes discussing Balzac, works by the use of antithesis, where opposite terms are kept in

circulation positioned against each other. Through the symbolic
code, definitions are mapped out: there is the sense of what range
of cultural or ideological possibilities the text is prepared to work
with.
3   The cultural code: this refers to the assumptions, the common currency of information that the writer can appeal to in
the reader: assumptions which are basic and represent received
opinion, or ideology. In the case of *Paradise Lost*, the incidents of
the Biblical narrative form a cultural code.

These codes are not to be taken as more than suggestive: they are
not to be applied mechanically. But take Lawrence's opening and
see if you can find examples of the five codes. When Barthes
discusses them, he divides the text up into fragments, or lexia, of
variable lengths (561 of these units of reading for Balzac's short
story *Sarrasine*). The point of making these divisions is to be able
to interrogate the text, not to succumb to the lure of narrative. I
do not want to copy Barthes, but you may find it interesting to
make your own divisions of the passage.

> *Fanny and Annie*
> Flame-lurid his face as he turned among the throng of flame-lit and
> dark faces upon the platform. In the light of the furnace she caught
> sight of his drifting countenance, like a piece of floating fire. And
> the nostalgia, the doom of homecoming went through her veins like
> a drug. His eternal face, flame-lit now! The pulse and darkness of
> red fire from the furnace towers in the sky, lighting the desultory,
> industrial crowds on the wayside station, lit him and went out.
>   Of course he did not see her. Flame-lit and unseeing! Always the
> same, with his meeting eyebrows, his common cap, and his red-
> and-black scarf knotted round his throat. Not even a collar to meet
> her! The flames had sunk, there was shadow.

DISCUSSION

1   The action code seems to me sustained through such linkings
as 'the platform' and 'the wayside station', the words 'turned',
'caught sight', 'meet', which work together to suggest the two
coming together – she from the train, he on the platform (and
coming together is a key action the text discusses). 'Of course'
suggests the woman knows the man, and that there is an element
of repetition, of familiarity, about the homecoming (itself a clue
word in the action code).
2   The hermeneutic code begins with the title: who are these two
women? Why are their names similar? How do the names relate to
the he and she in the extract? The sense of a mystery being set up
exists in the contrasts of light and shadow – 'flame-lit and dark

faces'; 'the pulse and darkness of red fire'; 'lit him and went out'; 'he did not see her. Flame-lit . . .'; 'The flames had sunk, there was shadow', versus the first 'Flame-lurid his face . . .'.

3 The semic code: character seems generated through the idea of his face being flame-lit (the faces of the others in shadow). Note 'his drifting countenance', 'his eternal face'; his face 'unseeing'; these words promote hermeneutic mystery, but also suggest a fascination about him, begun with the unusual 'Flame-lurid' – a description not repeated, but modified to the three-times repeated 'flame-lit'. Sexual, energetic and devilish connotations run through 'flame' (he is an 'old flame' of hers).

4 The symbolic code: the passage seems constructed on antitheses: he/she; light/dark; past/future in 'nostalgia' and 'homecoming'; the eternal/the momentary in 'the doom of homecoming' felt through the temporary sensation of a drug, or 'his *eternal* face, flame-lit *now*', and perhaps the furnace towers 'in the sky' versus the 'desultory, industrial crowd' on the platform; liquid/fire ('drifting countenance', 'floating fire', '. . . went through her veins like a drug').

5 The cultural code: the man meeting the woman; the dress of the workman versus polite clothing; a collar the signifier of respectability (he wears a red-and-black scarf: the colours fit the symbolism of fire and darkness).

These elements of coding go throughout the short story; they structure it. The conscious artistry of Lawrence intersects with an unconscious set of codings that generate familiar narrative possibilities and set up expectations that work on both the writer and the reader. Following Jakobson's definition of 'literariness',[5] the text can seek to de-familiarize the reader from the mental set produced through these codings; but that the codings are at work stresses the point that 'Fanny and Annie' is structured by more than the individual skill of the author. These codes keep the whole presentation in order, and they play in Lawrence's text.

How do these 'codes' of Barthes intersect with the elements of plot, character, narrator and narrative time that we have also looked at? Do they obviate the need for them? Are they reconcilable together as approaches? This question is not asked with the expectation that you can give anything like a final answer!

DISCUSSION

Clearly, Barthes's codes do not rule out the elements of writing identified by Aristotle: for example, the semic code meshes with ways of portraying character, and the proairetic and hermeneutic codes both fill in details of plot. Where the difference lies, I think, is in the question of intention and the author's consciousness of what is being done. Aristotle, and Leavis, in his analysis of 'Fanny and Annie' both think of the writer as the conscious artist. Barthes's codes point to layers that half construct a narration before the writer has got to work: in that sense, Barthes implies that narration and narratives surround us and form us before we mesh into them with our own desires and ways of thinking. The narratives that surround us are another aspect of ideology – of the common-sense assumptions that surround us.

So who is writing the narrative? According to a traditional criticism, the author, perhaps using the voice of a narrator. Barthes's codes, however, stress that another voice also speaks in the text: heard especially in the presuppositions of the cultural code, it is the voice of prevailing orthodoxy, of the dominant ideology at the heart of a society.

As a check on the points raised here, look at the following passage from the story:

> When Fanny sat at tea, her aunt, a grey-haired, fair-faced little woman, looked at her with an admiring heart, feeling bitterly sore for her. For Fanny was beautiful: tall, erect, finely coloured, with her delicately arched nose, her rich brown hair, her lustrous grey eyes. A passionate woman – a woman to be afraid of. So proud, so inwardly violent! She came of a violent race.
>
> It needed a woman to sympathize with her. Men had not the courage. Poor Fanny! She was such a lady, and so straight and magnificent. And yet everything seemed to do her down. Every time she seemed to be doomed to humiliation and disappointment, this handsome, brilliantly sensitive woman, with her nervous, over-wrought laugh.
>
> (p. 211)

In this fragment of the text, what different narratives and possibilities of narrative are there? Can you relate Barthes's codes to them? Can you use these to illuminate your sense of character, plot, narrator and narrative time?

DISCUSSION

1 The aunt narrativized as motherly, supportive, experienced; but also fair-faced: not mature, a little naive. Reliance on the semic code. Tea as a kind of gentility: the cultural code.
2 Fanny's character – passionate, proud, inwardly violent, a lady, straight, magnificent, handsome, brilliantly sensitive. Again the semic code. 'Overwrought' raises the element of mystery, but

certainly suggests that the narrative is taking up an attitude to Fanny, that it is seeing her as too sensitive, too refined (the rest of the narrative will destroy this trait in her).

3 A narrative of Fanny's past − 'Every time she seemed to be doomed to humiliation and disappointment'. This again breaks with narrative time: it is a flashback, covering Fanny's past. 'Seemed to be' suggests the hermeneutic code (what will happen to her this time?).

4 A narrative of the destiny of sensitive, nervous, overwrought women, confronted by inadequate men, who are narrativized as lacking 'courage'. Itself, that raises the hermeneutic code; will Harry turn out to have courage? Here the text relies on cultural assumptions about women. (The 'new woman' − the Suffragette − is quite near to the narrative portrayal here.) This involves the proairetic code and the hermeneutic one in a small way. Here the ideology of the text seems to come closest to surfacing: in the sense that a woman who is a 'lady' is actually over-refined and does not require sympathy. Strongly ideological feelings about women operate to reduce Fanny's 'violence'.

5 A narrative comparing the two women − one little, one tall, one grey-haired, one with 'rich brown hair', the aunt 'fair-faced' and Fanny 'finely coloured'. They complement each other: this stresses 'it needed a woman to sympathize'. One drinks tea, the other looks on and thinks admiringly (action code). Note the breaking of a time sequence to give the aunt's thoughts, which are not separate from Fanny's (e.g. the word 'doomed' is Fanny's or the narrator's − see the first paragraph of the story). The narrative suggests that this intimacy between the two will have to be broken. The combination of antithetical values seems to arise from the symbolic code. Other uses of the symbolic code here might include: female passion versus male pusillanimity; being a lady versus humiliation; sensitiveness versus ordinariness; richness and lustre (in the eyes and hair) versus being 'done down'.

6 As a variant on the cultural code, what of the grey eyes and the 'violent race'? It is possible that these may be unconscious references back to another Slavic heroine called Annie: to Tolstoy's *Anna Karenina*, a text Lawrence reacted strongly towards. Is there a further code here of *intertextuality*, whereby certain references are only explained by the reliance on certain well-known texts, texts whose assumptions themselves are part of people's way of thinking, however unconsciously?

Some comments on this: it is difficult to distinguish between these codes (in particular that the cultural code is dependent on the semic: that perception of a person's character e.g. as motherly, or passionate, requires a sense of the customs and conventions of the time). I think it is right to feel that the codes overlap, and that each code is explained by another. Barthes's point is that writing draws on unconscious assumptions and these structure the text, unless the writer tries to distort their operation. This becomes clear when considering the workings of the symbolic code. The contrast between the passionate woman and the weak man, for instance, seems to write itself. Once one term has been thought up, the other seems to follow. These oppositions, which seem natural and seem to dictate their own terms, are cultural, part of a conventional way of thinking that is so automatic and so much provoking an instant antithetical response that they are passed off as natural and spontaneous ways of thinking. That is a working definition of ideology.[6]

Lastly, why are the title names virtually the same? – Fanny, a near-rhyme with Harry, being Annie with an F? Fanny, at least from the time of *Fanny Hill* (1749) has had sexual associations: in the first paragraph of the story, note how often the text foregrounds the letter 'f' at the start of words: a letter itself with certain obvious low associations. Is the irony that Fanny is actually somebody strongly, if unconsciously, sexual? Is there a playing with the letter f in the first paragraph, itself partly unconscious at the level of the author's intention? This textual play at the level of language (the signifier) rather than just at the level of meaning (the signified) suggests that even discussion of the text in terms of codes may be inadequate – as indeed, Barthes's own movement in criticism from 'The Structural Analysis of Narrative' and *S/Z* to later work implies. However, the work on codes remains highly important too!

3. Who Narrates? Part 1

> By narrative we mean all those literary works which are dis-
> tinguished by two characteristics: the presence of a story and a
> story-teller.
>
>   Robert Scholes and Robert Kellogg, *The Nature of Narrative*
>   (OUP, 1966)

Consider this definition of narrative: does a narrative imply a
'story', and is there always a story-teller?

Is drama narrative? It doesn't usually have a story-teller,
apart, say, from the Chorus who narrates in Elizabethan tragedy,
or perhaps when a messenger gives an account of something
happening off-stage. We could argue that stage settings and cos-
tumes act indirectly as narrators; e.g. oppressively and heavily
furnished drawing rooms in Ibsen plays give hints of the stuffiness
of middle-class repression at work. Could drama be described as
narrative carried forward by a series of narrators (the characters)?
What of film? Is the camera the narrator there? Opera uses a
narrator in the music that accompanies actions: Wagnerian leit-
motifs certainly provide a narrator's intervention: background
music in films provides what Barthes would call a 'vertical intervention' in the onward linear flow of the story-line. But Aristotle
saw drama as opposed to narrative, in not using a narrator.
Scholes and Kellogg's argument follows on from this. They think
of oral, folk narratives and later written narratives where a narrator
is clearly relevant.

Narratology (the study of narratives), a term used first by
Tzvetan Todorov in 1969, dates from the pioneering work of
Vladimir Propp, whose *Morphology of the Folktale* (1928, but not
translated into English until 1958, which delayed its impact),
works on narratives with a traditional content: this content – the
action – being the *fabula*. Each different way the *fabula* is told

yields a different *sjuzet*. The linguist Emile Benveniste makes a distinction between the story and the way it is told in order to draw attention to the presence of a narrator's voice, with its distinct 'angle' on the events. Claude Bremond takes the Russian Formalist distinction associated with Propp amongst others, and translates it as *récit* and *raconté*; the second term encompassing both the *sjuzet* and the way it is told. The work of Gerard Genette establishes three terms: *story* (the totality of the narrated events), *narrative* (the discourse, oral or written, that narrates them), and *narrating* (the real or fictive act that produces that discourse – in other words the very fact of recounting). The last term, the narrating, again draws attention to the narrator.[1] I set this out as a table:

FORMALISTS: *fabula/sjuzet*
BENVENISTE: story/discourse – i.e. *histoire/discours*
BREMOND: *récit/raconté*
GENETTE: story/narrative/narrating

From this summary, we can distinguish four main points made by narratology:

1   A story can take numerous forms, and there is a distinction to be observed between the story and the actual text we have in front of us.
2   What alters our perception of a story may be the determination to see it as a plot (as Forster thought), but more crucially it is the presence of a narrator.
3   The analysis of the narrative, for Genette, following Todorov, involves consideration of the tenses,[2] aspect ('the way in which the story is perceived by the narrator') and mood ('the type of discourse used by the narrator') – *Narrative Discourse Revisited*, p. 29.
4   The whole narration, what Genette's work calls the 'narrating' – 'the producing narrative action, . . . the whole of the real or fictional situation in which that action takes place' (*Narrative Discourse Revisited*, p. 27) is to be studied: to put it at its simplest, the fact that a narrator is telling a story is itself a fact for investigation.

The narrator is crucial for narratology, and returning to our opening point, this means that drama is not narrative (so Genette). We will return to this problem, but first, consider the role of the narrator who alters the *fabula*.

What does the narrator do to make the work a narrative and not a drama? Aristotle's teacher, Plato (427–347 BC), in the

Republic iii. 393a establishes a distinction between the writer
representing or imitating the speech of another, and reporting
what happened. *Mimesis* (representation, simulation) happens
when a character's speech is rendered as it was said – as, for
instance, speeches enclosed in inverted commas, or speech in
drama. *Diegesis* is the narrator's simple account of what happened. Turning direct speech into reported speech turns mimesis
into diegesis. Drama is mimesis: epic narrative uses mimesis and
diegesis. The distinction between the two terms is itself unsatis-
factory, as Genette suggests, when he argues that actually all
art is representation (mimesis): nothing else than representation
according to conventions.[3]

In what follows, distinguish between author and narrator: a
distinction common in criticism since the 1950s. The narrator,
who says 'I' in the text, whose voice is implied in the manner in
which the story is told, is a dramatization made by the author, a
rhetorical performance. We begin with texts showing how much
to the forefront the narrator is. The first example comes from
very near the beginning of Fielding's conversationally-narrated
Tom Jones, and the writer takes advantage of the fact that he is
working in a comparatively new art-form, the novel, where he can
lay down some rules. Both the second and fourth examples are
the beginnings of last chapters, and so are concerned with the
question of how to end. The third opens a narrative and the fifth
comes from the middle of a novel, where a new character,
Dr Lydgate, is being introduced.

**Examine (a) how the narrator presents himself/herself: what
sort of person is implied? (b) What kind of reader is assumed?
What attitudes is the reader expected to have? (c) What relationship is set up between narrator and reader?**

1

Reader, I think proper, before we proceed any further together, to
acquaint thee, that I intend to digress, through this whole history,
as often as I see occasion: of which I am myself a better judge than
any pitiful critic whatever. And here I must desire all those critics to
mind their own business, and not to intermeddle with affairs, or
works, which no ways concern them. . . .
(Henry Fielding: *The History of Tom Jones* (1749) Book 1, Ch. 2)

2

Let other pens dwell on guilt and misery. I quit such odious subjects
as soon as I can, impatient to restore every body, not greatly in
fault themselves, to tolerable comfort, and to have done with all
the rest.
    My Fanny, indeed, at this very time, I have the satisfaction of
knowing, must have been happy in spite of every thing. She must

have been a happy creature in spite of all that she felt, or thought she felt, for the distress of those around her.

(Jane Austen: *Mansfield Park* (1814) Ch. 48)

3

Marley was dead, to begin with. There is no doubt whatever about that. The register of his burial was signed by the clergyman, the clerk, the undertaker and the chief mourner. Scrooge signed it. And Scrooge's name was good upon 'Change, for anything he chose to put his hand to.

Old Marley was as dead as a doornail.

Mind! I don't mean to say that I know, of my own knowledge, what there is particularly dead about a doornail. I might have been inclined, myself, to regard a coffin-nail as the deadest piece of ironmongery in the trade. But the wisdom of our ancestors is in the simile; and my unhallowed hands shall not disturb it, or the country's done for. You will therefore allow me to repeat emphatically, that Marley was as dead as a doornail.

Scrooge knew he was dead? Of course he did.

(Charles Dickens: *A Christmas Carol* (1843) Stave One)

4

Reader, I married him. A quiet wedding we had ...

(Charlotte Brontë: *Jane Eyre: An Autobiography* (1847) Ch. 38)

5

The man [Dr Lydgate] was still in the making ... and there were both virtues and faults capable of shrinking or expanding. The faults will not, I hope, be a reason for the withdrawal of your interest in him. Among our valued friends is there not some one or other who is a little too self-confident and disdainful; whose distinguished mind is a little spotted with commonness; who is a little pinched here and protuberant there with native prejudices; or whose better energies are liable to lapse down the wrong channel under the influence of transient solicitations?

(George Eliot: *Middlemarch* (1871) Ch. 15)

DISCUSSION

1 The story-teller establishes himself as on a common footing with the reader: we are 'proceeding together' with the narrator, who confidently addresses the reader in the confidence that there is only one sort of reader, and that it is different from the class of 'critics'. The announcement of the intention to digress means the text is being recognized as a fiction, as something that can be started and stopped at will: in classing it as a fiction, note the contrast apparent in that the text is called a 'history' (note the full title): a history implies a narrative which is not a fiction, which links things up causally, as a plot.

The 'I' who stands in for the author is not Fielding, but a projection, a self-dramatization of an eighteenth-century man of leisure; a club-man, who is going at a leisurely pace, his own speed, and is consciously flouting the opinions of professional writers. So long as we remember that this is a presentation of the self in the text, we shall not call him simply 'Fielding'.

2   The narrator here draws attention to herself as deliberately manipulating the fiction she is writing. As with *Tom Jones*, there is the assumption that the fiction can be changed at will, according to the taste of the narrator. The narrator presents herself as the writer of a particular type of fiction: perhaps suggesting that writers who dwell on guilt and misery are guilty of bad taste. Thus the text aims to get the reader into alignment with the attitudes of the narrator. Or perhaps the narrator assumes a modesty here. In which case, is the modesty deliberate or assumed, part of a self-projection? Is the voice here assumed to be male or female?

3   With this opening of Dickens's first 'Christmas Book', the narrator, who imitates Fielding in his willingness to digress, wishes to present himself as a jocular, friendly figure, telling a story to an intimate circle of friends. The readers as an *audience* are assumed in 'You will therefore permit me to repeat', as though the words were spoken, not written, and a reader's voice is assumed to have been heard, licensing the reply 'Scrooge knew he was dead? Of course he did', which is deliberately familiar, but so is the 'chatty' tone of the digression about the doornail. The narrator sounds certain – 'there is no doubt whatever' and 'emphatically', but this is playfulness: starting a ghost story (the chapter title is 'Marley's Ghost'); for we know, despite being brow-beaten by the friendly narrator, that though Marley is dead, he will make an appearance.

4   This text is different from the others in that the narrator is given a name, Jane Eyre. The title, *Jane Eyre: An Autobiography, edited by Currer Bell* presents the idea of a woman's text being edited by a man, for Currer Bell was initially assumed by the London publishers to be male, and there was room for doubt whether the words being read were by Jane Eyre or Currer Bell. But this opening of the last chapter makes it clear that the text is fiction, not autobiography, or autobiography rendered as fiction. 'Reader, I married him' is a comforting line for those who like to read the last chapter first, as many readers do. Something of the same spirit of reassurance to readers who like a happy ending is apparent in *Mansfield Park*. The reader is perhaps assumed to be a person who likes romance, and wants a happy ending: a confidence is assumed with this reader by the narrator, Jane Eyre,

who is a disguise for the narrator, who is herself (or remembering Currer Bell, himself) a disguise or dramatization of Charlotte Brontë.

5 Again, the author has adopted a mask – George Eliot – a name which initially made some people think the author was male (not Marian Evans). But again, the narrator is not to be identified with Marian Evans: the narrator remains a projection, a person of liberal views, addressing the readership on friendly, though dignified terms – 'I hope' for instance strikes a tone of earnestness, of non-'transient solicitation'. At this point Doctor Lydgate, idealist in medicine, but 'spotted with commonness' when it comes to relationships with women, is being described, and the narrator is about to be highly critical of him. The reader is pulled up lest he or she should be too dismissive; in which case, such a reader would join the list of valued friends who are too self-confident and disdainful. The passage, in fact is about the reader as much as about the reader's friends – friends like those the narrator has – and many readers have found the moral certainty implied objectionable, even if witty.

Note that the intervention of the narrator telling us about future faults which are to be revealed again draws attention to the fictionality of the work: the sense of the narrator and reader in a compact together, agreeing with each other, as much as Fielding assumes that there will be such agreement.

In each of the passages, the narrator's presence is complemented by a reader's. Fielding and Brontë both refer openly to the reader: each of the other texts assumes a debate being conducted with the imagined reader (the 'narratee'). Behind Fielding is Cervantes' *Don Quixote* (1604–1615), which opens with 'The Author's Preface to the Reader' (itself a parody piece: a preface about how to write a preface, consisting mainly of an imaginary conversation between 'Cervantes' (the author's self-projection) and a friend). The reader addressed in the first line is the 'desocupado lector' – the idle reader.

What does this imply? That novelistic narrative, belonging to a print culture, projects a fixed, definite private reader, or a reader as part of a fixed circle, like the family one in Dickens. The term the 'narratee' implicitly accepts this placing of the reader, who is invited to interpret and complete the text – and that the writer regards the reader as an individual. It is a powerful way of creating the reader as the responsible, if passive agent who exists in a timeless relationship with the author. For the existence of the reader seems to make the author more powerful, more

individual as a presence. There is an anxiety to preserve or create
an imaginary unity, disregarding the actual differences between
elements in an audience or readership.

George Eliot and Ideology

Fielding expects to take the reader with him in opposition to the
critics, and George Eliot tries to create and secure the readership
she wants: one which will agree with her views and respect her
especially when she is professing an agnosticism, an uncertainty
about which of two positions is the right path to follow; a characteristic move in her fiction. The passage quoted may be said to
interpellate the reader. Interpellation is one of the most useful
terms derived from the work of Louis Althusser, the Marxist
philosopher whose work on ideology discusses its role in securing
the consent of exploited people to their own subjection and to the
rule (hegemony) of others. Althusser defines ideology by saying
that by it 'men represent their real conditions to themselves in an
imaginary form'.[4] Pause over this definition. **What is the difference between 'real conditions' and 'imaginary form'? Does the
definition illuminate the concept of narrative?**

DISCUSSION

People's 'real conditions' are their actual circumstances. The
'imaginary form' refers to the idealized way in which these circumstances are interpreted.

In the definition, the word 'represent' could well be replaced
by 'narrate'. To represent to someone why I am the worker
and this other person the boss, for instance, immediately involves stories and the setting out of relationships. Narration *is* a
'representation' of things as they are. But the word 'representation' implies we are not seeing the real thing, but only an
imitation, or copy, or image or symbol of it, so a narration cannot
deal 'straight' with reality, but can only give a picture of it. The
picture that ideology offers is idealized; it belongs to the realm of
the 'imaginary'. Althusser refers to the psychoanalyst Jacques
Lacan, who discusses the idealized self-perception the child gains
in the 'mirror phase', a vision of a *je-idéal* that is whole, larger
than life and self-possessed. The point is that the imaginary form,
the representation that appeals to the narcissistic sense of the
narrator and the reader, conditions and structures narrative representation. But it probably cannot succeed in doing this fully. To
what extent narrative simply fits ideology – or is – ideological is
the subject of this *Guide*.

In narration, the story-teller represents conditions both for his or her own benefit, and also for the benefit of those hearing or reading. Now it may be that the narrator deliberately tries to mislead his or her readers, which is not what Althusser is talking about, but it is more common that an author is not himself/herself fully aware of the conditions described; may be held by the imaginary position in a series of mis-recognitions. Readers are also already positioned by ideological beliefs, so that they read the texts in a way which accords with their own ideological assumptions.

Althusser calls the process by which ideology 'grabs' people interpellation. 'All ideology hails or interpellates concrete individuals as concrete subjects' (p. 162). Interpellation is like someone calling out, 'Hey, you there' in the street. When the hailed individual turns round, 'by this mere one-hundred-and-eighty-degree physical conversion, he becomes a subject' (p. 163). The person imagines the call is directed to him/her personally, and by reacting, becomes subject to it and to the person calling out. So, when George Eliot refers to 'our valued friends', the reader's response may be to think that the text is making a virtually personal address. But certainly George Eliot was not writing for anyone in the 1990s. Interpellation explains how the lure of narrative, for instance, unconsciously gathers readers into the value-system, beliefs and ideology of the narrator.

Behind the narrator stands an ideology which has interpellated him/her. The narrator as a character is already caught into a misrepresentation of the real conditions of existence. For example, when Fielding's narrator dismisses critics, does this point to an ideology that considers life can be understood in common-sense, untheorized terms – purely empirically? In *Middlemarch*, what of the contrasting of 'the distinguished mind' with 'commonness'? Is there an ideology here, where certain states of mind are dismissible as unworthy – as 'common' (inevitably a word with class-associations)? In examples 2 and 4, what do the attitudes to happy endings imply in terms of an ideology of marriage and the family? What attitudes to the past and to tradition mark out the Dickens extract? What of the assumption in the second extract that the novelist/narrator knows better than Fanny how she really felt about the tragedies of wasted lives and loves, in *Mansfield Park*? Isn't this a projecting of feelings on to the character, which is actually creating her as a subject of that system of values? Ideology may also prevent the writer from seeing certain things. When the narrator in *Mansfield Park* declares that she will not speak of such odious matters as guilt and misery, is this a voluntary refusal, or an unconscious marker that there are certain things that a woman in her society cannot know and is unable to treat? So she plays down Fanny's sympathy, as though protecting her own space, which is actually a lack of liberty, of ability to see, since she is caught by an imaginary representation of how things are.

The Narrator and the Author

Can we get from the narrator to the author behind the narrator? The narrator's ideology may be at a distance from the author's in cases where the narrator is presented for criticism: or where the narrator is presented as unreliable, but it is more common for people to argue that the views of the narrator in *Middlemarch* will accord with those of Marian Evans. But the narrator should never be given more status than that of a character in the text. The narrator is a carefully stage-managed effect. Further, what is the difference between a narrator who says 'I', as in *A Christmas Carol*, and a hero or heroine who says 'I', like Jane Eyre? Very little, apart from the extent that the narrator is embodied: we know more of Jane Eyre than we do of the narrator in Fielding; though even this is contestable. It might be better to say that a narrator is present in all texts: the question is to what extent the narrator is drawn attention to. That there is a narrator who could say 'I' seems evident in fictional texts: whether the word 'I' actually appears or not is not so important; it is almost an accident, if it does, since both the existence and the direction of the narrative imply a narrator. In 'Fanny and Annie' we get 'Let us confess it at once' (pp. 209, 176). Even in this narrative, where there are so many points of view which appear unattributed, a narrator is at work. (Look again at that paragraph from 'Fanny and Annie', and compare it with the first Dickens extract given above.) To quote Genette: 'insofar as the narrator can at any time intervene *as such* in the narrative, every narrating is, by definition, . . . presented in the first person' (*Narrative Discourse*, p. 244).

But if all narration is implicitly first person, it might also be argued that by the same token *no* narrative is in essence the voice of an author; no narrative necessarily takes us back to an author's experience and attitudes. In contrast to the earlier examples in this chapter of a narrative voice, take this piece, complete in itself, from the Argentine novelist, Jorge Luis Borges (1899–1986). It reads like a playful (perhaps) confession – or a declaration of inadequacy – but who is narrating? And who is he describing? What is the point of the last line?

Borges and I

It's to the other, to Borges, that things occur. I walk through Buenos Aires and linger, perhaps mechanically by now, to look at an arched entrance and its wrought-iron door; I get news of Borges through the post and I see his name among three professors on a ballot sheet or in a biographical dictionary. I like hourglasses, maps, eighteenth-century typography, etymologies, the flavour of coffee and the prose of Stevenson; the other shares these choices, but in a showy way which transforms them into the attributes of an actor. It would be too much to assert that our relationship is hostile; I live, I let myself live, so that Borges can devise his literature, and that literature justifies me. I am willing to confess that he has brought off a few worthwhile pages, but those pages cannot save me, perhaps because the good in them no longer belongs to anyone, not even to the other, but to language and tradition. Apart from this, I am destined to be lost, definitively, and only a few instants of me will be able to live on in the other. Little by little, everything is yielding to him, although I am well aware of his perverse habit of falsifying and overstating. Spinoza held that all things wish to persist in their being; the stone eternally wishes to be a stone, the tiger a tiger. I have to remain in Borges, not in myself (if indeed I am someone), but I recognise myself less in his books than in many others, or in the strenuous flourish on a guitar. Years ago I tried to free myself from him, and I passed from the myths of the city's edge to games with time and infinity, but these games belong to Borges and I will have to think up something else. Thus my life is in flight, and I lose everything, to oblivion or to the other.

I do not know which of the two is writing this page.[5]

DISCUSSION

What is the status of this narrator? The last line declares that he is not in control, not authoritative. He declares himself subsidiary to 'Borges', who seems to be taking him over, perhaps as 'George Eliot' takes Marian Evans over in people's imaginations.

A suggested interpretation: the speaker/writer feels himself double. Is that why Stevenson is mentioned, as the author of *Dr Jekyll and Mr Hyde* – a famous story about just this problem? Perhaps the identical middle names of the two writers is also relevant. Perhaps the activity of writing creates a new self – a 'Borges', who has author-status, fame and public attention, but whose increasingly separate existence seems to be destroying the self who writes, who cannot keep up with what has been created. He is reduced to a mechanical passivity, aware of the circulation of his name in a separate space. At the same time, the self that has been created is fixed: he is called Borges. He seems to take over from the other Borges, and appears as a kind of parody of him. It is not authors who create writing, but writing creates the 'author', henceforth called 'Borges' – given a stable, fixed identity.

The word 'I' turns out to be plural, to refer to more than one self. 'I' is an example of *deixis*. That is, words such as today, tomorrow, then, now, I, you, have no agreed objective meaning; they are deictic. Wednesday is today for me now, but Thursday will be today tomorrow. I and you are *shifters* in Roman Jakobson's terms: words with a meaning which changes according to the user. Emile Benveniste distinguishes, in speech, between the 'subject of the *énoncé*' (statement) and the 'subject of the *énonciation*' – the person who speaks – between the 'I' who speaks in a sentence, as in 'I am starved' and the I who says that. The speaking 'I' projects a self who is starved; in actuality, the 'I' is much more than starved (or perhaps not even that hungry at all) and the non-coincidence between the speaking I and the subject I who is spoken, sets up a difference between author and created 'I' within the text. If I say 'I am a liar', the statement does not necessarily mean that the first 'I' is actually lying and that the statement is untrue: there remains a gap between the 'I' saying that and the 'I' in the sentence 'I am a liar.'[6] When we talk to ourselves – most people do, though few like to admit it! – the 'other' addressed is interchangeably 'I' or 'you'. Moments like these suggest that the 'I' is not single or stable, or even plainly referential, just as it looks as though the claim of some linguists that language is for communication is baffled by the idea that we spend words on talking to 'another' 'I'.

If the 'I' in narrative is purely deictic, a shifter, there is no coincidence between the author and the narrator. In 'Borges and I', whoever speaks feels he is being lost as a result of a mysterious 'they' – the literal translation of 'everything is yielding to him' is 'they are yielding him everything'. It is not even just a question of becoming double: the three names on the ballot sheet (perhaps Borges, Borges and Borges) is surely suggestive that 'the other' is not simply a fixed single identity that has been created. The 'I' that speaks in the text, the subject of the *énoncé*, is himself a fictional construct written out by – whoever. He is not the original Borges.

We could conclude that in considering narrative, it is not helpful either to dwell upon the ostensible narrator, or to posit a relationship between that artefact and the 'author', and to start talking about the 'author's intentions' or the 'author's meaning', as though these were matters that could be spoken about with some definition. **Is autobiography any better, where the author is supposed to be writing about his/her life? Have we encountered autobiography before in this *Guide*?**

DISCUSSION

Yes – in the title *Jane Eyre: An Autobiography*. But this not only traps us in a number of possible narrators (Brontë/Currer Bell/ Jane Eyre), and presents us with a life which is actually only fictional, but it makes the whole idea of what is an autobiography undecidable. (Most readers of the novel agree that there are some details in it which are drawn from Charlotte Brontë's own life: does that substantiate it as autobiography?) And 'Borges and I' is also autobiography – but we could not be sure from reading it that we have reliable information about the Argentine novelist. It would not prove a safe basis for a biography. The details about Borges' likes sound like journalistic gossip, complicit in the ideology of what a famous author is like (an aesthete, a dilettante, somebody totally useless). 'Borges and I' suggests that however much an author may wish to lay bare his/her soul, a different self is created in the text. *Jane Eyre* does not even allow us to take the word 'autobiography' literally. I leave on one side the assumption in autobiographical writing that the subject of the *énonciation* is in a position to recognize the 'truth' of his/her own situation, while being framed by an ideology.

Conclusion

We have looked at the distinction between author and narrator, and examined how narrative interpellates the reader into certain positions of near-passive agreement to an ideological position. We have considered whether the terms 'mimesis' and 'diegesis' help in discussing narrative, or cause trouble by assuming the presence of a narrator – a presence which itself may only be an effect of the way something is written (writing generates the impression that there is a narrator). With 'Borges and I', and with the issue of deixis, we have considered not only how the narrator and the author cannot be regarded as identical, but also how narrative cannot give a single unambiguous account of the views and attitudes of the 'I' who writes. In other words, perhaps it is a mistake to think that a narrative renders the isolatable views of a story-teller?

4. Who Narrates? Part 2

Writing [is] the destruction of every voice, or every point of origin.
Writing is that neutral, composite, oblique space where our subject
slips away, the negative where all identity is lost.
                              (Roland Barthes: 'The death of the author')

Go back to the opening of Chapter 3, Scholes and Kellogg's
definition of narrative. Compare this with the above passage from
Barthes. We have come a long way from Scholes and Kellogg –
however 'commonsensical' their view, every aspect of their definition needs challenging. Barthes, notice, uses the word 'writing'
to get away from the idea of texts comprising definable narratives
constituted by the existence of a story-teller. He is close to 'Borges
and I' which suggests that in writing, the good in it 'no longer
belongs to anyone'. Writing cannot speak of an author, or lead us
back to an author. As 'Borges and I' finishes, 'I do not know
which of the two is writing this page'. Hence the phrase Barthes
uses, 'the death of the author'. Instead of writing perpetuating the
certain, distinctive views of a writer like George Eliot, it divides us
from them.

Roland Barthes argues for the death of the author, because he
wants to uncouple the text from the ideological commitments of
the historical author. We must return to this point, but first
consider how the idea of 'the author' is one that itself serves an
ideological function.

In the early modern narrative, *Don Quixote* (part 1 1605,
part 2 1615), Cervantes (1547–1616) is very self-conscious about
the concept of the author. He begins with a Preface (referred to in
Chapter 3) in which he describes himself as unable to write a
preface, and thus ready to give up the whole book until 'a certain
friend of mine' appears and tells him what to write and how to
write it, which Cervantes relates as the Preface, with no more

added. In other words, he splits himself into two, in a way very similar to 'Borges and I'. He then opens the narrative with eight chapters which he breaks off suddenly, saying that the original author gave up at this point. He describes himself as only the 'second undertaker' of the work, unable to believe that the 'history' stops there. In the next chapter he describes how he found in a bazaar the account of Don Quixote given by the Arab Cid Hamet Benengeli, and continues it saying that he is only translating Cid Hamet, and the reader must remember that Cid Hamet was a liar. In Part 2 of the novel, the author in his Preface protests against the existence of a fake *Don Quixote* which had appeared in novel form in 1614. The first chapter of Part 2 begins with the assertion that Cid Hamet is again being followed, that the author is only the translator. We read of Don Quixote and his friends discussing the accounts that have already been circulated of his adventures. They read that Cid Hamet is looking to find out how the narrative continued, and with much scorn for the fictitiousness of what they expect Cid Hamet will write, Don Quixote and Sancho Panza go on knight-errantry once more.

What is the importance of this new stress on authorship? What ideological importance is there in talking about the author? – instead of merely saying that Cervantes has written the text? You need to think of the implications of designating somebody as an 'author'.

DISCUSSION

There seem to me four reasons:

1 Since Cervantes attacked imitators, he stressed the author's uniqueness and the text's: it is original, the product of the writer's genius or talent.
2 Cervantes effectively plays on the fiction that the author is independent of ideology, of his age and separate from other writers who are working in the same field. 'The *explanation* of a work is always sought in the man or woman who produced it, as if it were in the end, through the more or less transparent allegory of the fiction, the voice of a single person, the *author* confiding in us.'[1]
3 The idea of the author builds up the idea of a unique relationship between story-teller as a virtually knowable person, and reader.
4 The belief in the single author encourages a sense that truth and knowledge lie within one person's vision, their empirical observation, and can be passed on to the reader.

Thus in Fielding, indebted to Cervantes, and in Austen, Dickens, Brontë, Eliot and Lawrence – writers we have concentrated on so far – the author, through the narrator, feels confident enough to tell readers the significance of what happens, assured that they will follow the point. In each text, the narrator stands at the centre of the text, which is 'non-focalized' (Genette). In non- or zero-focalized narration, the narrator is omniscient. Fielding's digressions show his confidence in his ability to direct attention, to describe and analyse things as they are, to give a perfect mimesis. For example, in *A Christmas Carol* the narrator describes Scrooge being visited by the Ghost of Christmas Past:

> The curtains of his bed were drawn aside, I tell you, by a hand. Not the curtains at his feet, nor the curtains at his back, but those to which his face was addressed. The curtains of his bed were drawn aside; and Scrooge, starting up into a half-recumbent attitude, found himself face to face with the unearthly visitor, who drew them: as close to it as I am now to you, and as I am standing in the spirit at your elbow.
>
> (Stave Two)

Go back to the earlier Dickens extract (p. 29) to see how this passage is similar to it. Is interpellation functioning here? Can you comment on the significance of the narrator's desire to insist on his presence in the text, and his deliberate alignment of himself (via the word 'spirit') with the Ghost of Christmas Past?

DISCUSSION

The first question should be easy. In both extracts the narrator presents events as though they were objective facts. This kind of writing belongs to the prevalent nineteenth-century realist mode. The narrator wishes to be as close to his readership as the Ghost is to Scrooge; the illusion is maintained that reader and writer are on the same level, the reader interpellated into exactly the narrator's position.

Thus the narrator aligns himself with the Ghost of Christmas Past (and with all the spirits of the *Carol*), and their function, to show Scrooge his past, present and future, may well symbolize the realist writer's work – telling ('I tell you') and showing people what they are like, calling up reality before their eyes. Perhaps the effect of comparing himself to the Ghost of Christmas Past is to interpellate the reader in a double way, firstly as beside the Ghost, seeing as it sees; secondly, perhaps, as Scrooge. The middle-class readers of 1843 are invited to see themselves in this light: this certainly fits with the note of social protest running through the text. (Dickens is alien from one aspect of his society's ideology: its public meanness and its doctrine of self-help.) The first inter-pellation encourages readers to think they are getting the whole story: that the novelist is keeping nothing back.

The Author and Indirect Free Discourse

The realist writer sometimes imposes an author's point of view more indirectly than by simply 'telling' the reader. Near the end of the chapter the Ghost shows Scrooge, in a flashback, a party from which he, as a then younger man, had excluded himself. In the party games, where much flirtation takes place, the narrator adds:

> What would I not have given to be one of them? Though I never could have been so rude, no, no! I wouldn't for the wealth of all the world have crushed that braided hair, and torn it down; as for the precious little shoe, I wouldn't have plucked it off, God bless my soul! to save my life ... And yet I should have dearly liked, I own, to touch her lips. . . .

Suspend comments on these male fantasies, and note that Scrooge is not among the merry-makers. At the end (Stave Five), on Christmas Day, the converted Scrooge shows up at his nephew's party. Unexpected, he knocks on the door.

> 'Is your master at home, my dear?' said Scrooge to the girl. Nice girl! Very!

Who says 'Nice girl'? The narrator, obviously, but it would seem also to be what Scrooge thinks. If so, it provides a model of a typical movement towards closure in the realist text: the charac-ters concurring in the judgements of the author-like narrator. The attitude to the servant answering the door is the same as the narrator's to the women at the party: to think like the narrator is the mark of Scrooge's conversion, indeed. And if Scrooge provides an imaginary model for readers to recognize themselves in, it could be said that the model for narrative in the realist text is the gradual bringing of focal characters and readers into line with the point of view expressed in the text. This is almost exactly the meaning of closure – a term met with in Chapter 2 and to which we return in the next chapter.

This kind of closure works with the detective novel, which may be regarded as a paradigm of the realist text. The activity of reading brings the reader into the same way of thinking as the detective, whose controlling discourse models the narrator's: directing the reader's response to each of the characters in the novel. The detective appears to prove things by simple empirical methods, though actually he does not: the empiricism is deceptive, a sleight of hand is involved. But the appearance of a logical open-handed progression is there, bearing out the claim that 'a classic realist text may be defined as one in which there is a hierarchy amongst the discourses which compose the text, and this hierarchy is defined in terms of an empirical nature of truth'.[2]

With 'Nice girl! Very!' and the question of who speaks, the answer must be that the remark is unattributable, finally to one person: it is an example of indirect free discourse – narration where a statement goes beyond the particular reach of any one figure, and ambiguity is left as to whose point of view we are hearing. Examples of this can be seen in 'Fanny and Annie'. The very first sentence, 'Flame-lurid his face as he turned among the throng of flame-lit and dark faces upon the platform' is a case in point. Is this the narrator's point of view or Fanny's? It may be Fanny's, but would she use this language? Here is an example from the opening of Tolstoy's *Anna Karenina*. **Which sentence here is unattributable? Which assumes a narrator?**

> All happy families resemble one another, but each unhappy family is unhappy in its own way.
>   Everything was upset in the Oblonskys' house. The wife had discovered an intrigue between her husband and their former French governess...
>   (Leo Tolstoy: *Anna Karenina* (1877), trans. Aylmer Maude
>   (Oxford: 1939)

DISCUSSION

The first seems to be indirect free speech. The second begins the omniscient narrator's voice. To ask who speaks the first sentence is to realize that no single person need utter this generalization: it is the voice of a dominant viewpoint: of an orthodoxy about marriage and the family. It comes from the ideology of the society that *Anna Karenina* is part of, constructed by, in part.[3]

The novelist with which indirect free discourse is historically most associated is Gustave Flaubert (1821–70). His impact is felt with Henry James (1843–1916), whose work shows a changed direction from Dickens or George Eliot. James dismisses the tradition of a narrator being present in the fiction, confidently 'telling'. He insists on the text 'showing' by a process of dramatization. In the Preface (1908) to *The Portrait of a Lady* (1881), James describes his method: 'Place the centre of the subject in the young woman's own consciousness'. The inner behaviour and thoughts of a single consciousness, or a series of consciousnesses (as in *The*

Wings of the Dove, 1902) are to replace, as 'reflectors' (so he calls them in the Preface) the omniscient narrator. The narrative is focalized.

For an example of this method, take the opening of *The Wings of the Dove*. I have numbered each sentence, for easier commentary:

[1] She waited, Kate Croy, for her father to come in, but he kept her waiting unconscionably, and there were moments at which she showed herself, in the glass over the mantel, a face positively pale with the irritation that had brought her to the point of going away without sight of him. [2] It was at this point, however, that she remained; changing her place, moving from the shabby sofa to the armchair upholstered in a glazed cloth that gave at once – she had tried it – the sense of the slippery and of the sticky. [3] She had looked at the sallow prints on the walls and at the lonely magazine, a year old, that combined, with a small lamp in coloured glass and a knitted white centre-piece wanting in freshness, to enhance the effect of the purplish cloth on the principal table; she had above all, from time to time, taken a brief stand on the small balcony to which the pair of long windows gave access. [4] The vulgar little street, in this view, offered scant relief from the vulgar little room; its main office was to suggest to her that the narrow black house-fronts, adjusted to a standard that would have been low even for backs, constituted quite the publicity implied by such privacies. [5] One felt them in the room exactly as one felt the room – the hundred like it or worse – in the street. [6] Each time she turned in again, each time, in her impatience, she gave him up, it was to sound to a deeper depth, while she tasted the faint, flat emanation of things, the failure of fortune and of honour. [7] If she continued to wait it was really, in a manner, that she might not add the shame of fear, of individual personal collapse, to all the other shames. [8] To feel the street, to feel the room, to feel the table-cloth and the centre-piece and the lamp, gave her a small, salutary sense, at least, of neither shirking or lying. [9] This whole vision was the worst thing yet – as including, in particular, the interview for which she had prepared herself; and for what had she come but for the worst?

It is obvious that there is a narrator in this extract, but what of the consciousness of Kate Croy? Are there words and phrases which mark parts of the piece off as not the voice of an impersonal narrator?

DISCUSSION

Taking this sentence by sentence:

1 The word 'unconscionably': this seems Kate Croy's opinion of her father's delay.

2 'Shabby' may be her valuation; and the slippery and sticky chair is described as such on the basis of her having tried to sit there: she is probably right in her view of the tactile qualities of the furniture, but 'she had tried it' marks off the opinion as her own. The same comment applies to the description of the furniture in the next sentence.

3 'She had looked' and 'she had . . . taken a brief stand' could well be her enumeration of what she had done while waiting. See also the repetitions in sentences 4, 5, 6, and 8; all worth noting for this.

4 The word 'vulgar'. The repetition borrows from a characteristic method of description in Dickens, but the word seems to reflect her view and her state of mind. The snobbishness (the phrasing of 'adjusted to a standard that would be low even for backs') is hers, so too the smartness of 'quite the publicity implied by such privacies'; note 'quite' (measured contempt). Nonetheless the word-play goes beyond Kate Croy. The 'backs' are backs of houses and pun also on backs of dresses, so that 'low' is also a pun (low class and low cut – so inviting disapproval). This second meaning reintroduces the narrator. 'Backs' may well also be outside toilets. Kate Croy feels that the fronts publicize the privacies – the deprivations she feels in this room; she also feels the fronts are as mean and indecorous as the interior private spaces of the houses opposite; she feels the *black* fronts are all you would expect from such mean places, no better than *backs* (whose is this word-play?) perhaps she puns on 'privies' – the houses are no better than the toilets to their rear. While she is clearly sophisticated and a socialite, it is difficult to attribute this voice: perhaps it is free indirect discourse.

5 The tone of the previous sentence intensifies with the use of 'one': the sense of a languid drawl marks the passage off as her voice.

6 Here note the repeated 'each time', which suggests her mounting irritation, as though she is speaking; but 'in her impatience' is obviously not her point of view: it seems to be a narrator's. 'The failure of fortune and honour' (whose, her father's, or hers, is not stated) is a key phrase: it suggests her valuation of things, where 'fortune' may simply mean the loss of money, and honour may just mean status. But the phrase is so loaded and so 'literary' that it also leaves room for the reader to think of the moral losses (e.g. of honesty) that take place in this book: such a valuation (which implies a strong ideological commitment) seems to me clearly intended. 'Sound' includes 'sound off', which implies that in this word two different valuations are implied: the narrator's comment

on her tone of superiority, and her sense of degradation.
7,8 These sentences sound like her own rationalization. Why
does she stay at 'this point' (sentence 2)? Note the conversation in
'it was really, in a manner', and 'at least'.
9 The conversation rises to a climax with the rhetorical question,
and the sense of a conclusion: 'this whole vision'; note the paren-
thesis, which contains a self-dramatizing note: 'prepared herself'.

On the basis of this analysis, the first sentence seems like a stage-
direction. Out of that setting the scene, the voice of Kate Croy
emerges, taking over, reducing the narrator to an embodiment of
her emotional attitudes, reporting the 'I' as 'she', and changing the
tenses from present to past. The narrator as a 'telling' voice is
effaced. The scene is in part 'interior monologue', which Scholes
and Kellogg define as 'a direct, immediate presentation of the
unspoken thoughts of a character without any intervening narrator'
(p. 177).

Point of View

Percy Lubbock (1879–1965) in *The Craft of Fiction*[4] follows
James's arguments closely by saying that in *The Wings of the
Dove* 'there is next to no narrative at all' (p. 184); that all is
dramatized, by each character giving in turns their point of view:
mimesis, not diegesis, indeed.

A stress on 'point of view' marks James's and Lubbock's
turning away from the omniscient narrator, whom they tend to
identify with the author. Similarly Joseph Conrad in *Heart of
Darkness* (1899) rejects this narrator, by beginning with one
narrator who seems to be a dramatization of Conrad, but continuing with another, Marlow's: Marlow being widely taken as
Conrad's self-presentation. *Heart of Darkness* thus works as a
text without a centre, without a single point of view, split between
two consciousnesses, neither privileged over the other. This seems
the ground of 'Borges and I'. Realist texts of the nineteenth century
could often leave open the question as to how to interpret certain
events. But the events themselves were not questioned. James's
insistence on 'point of view' even puts events in doubt: it asks,
what, if anything, has taken place? The effacing of the narrator
means, Lubbock writes, 'this is not *my* story, says the author; you
know nothing of me; it is the story of this man or woman in
whose words you have it, and he or she is a person whom you *can*
know' (p. 174). The wish in Jamesian narrative is to make the
reader confront and 'watch constructively' (p. 170) the characters'
points of view. The text becomes an expression of agnosticism, as

with the last sentence of 'Borges and I'. The narrator who could provide some stability has left: gone are the certitudes of Fielding, or Austen. This emphasis on the reader's construction of narrative dislodges the author and his/her authority: it decentres a narrative where the author directs everything.

For Lubbock 'the art of fiction does not begin until the novelist thinks of his story as a matter to be shown, to be so exhibited that it will tell itself' (p. 62). The effacing of the narrator in some Modernist texts has gone along with the desire to keep the author out – to make the text impersonal. To quote James Joyce's Stephen Dedalus, 'The artist, like the God of creation, remains within or behind or beyond or above his handiwork, invisible, refined out of existence, indifferent, paring his fingernails'. So too T.S. Eliot argued that 'the progress of an artist is a continual self-sacrifice, a continual extinction of personality'.[5] The desire in Joyce is for a non-narrated narration, one without the intruding subjectivity of the writer. Indirect free discourse and the use of the interior monologue cut out the story-teller and make the scene more objectively presented, and open to the reader's interpretation.

Narrative and Ideology: Who Speaks?

Yet however much texts in the modern moment try to be free of authorial control, can that free them from an ideological formation? I would argue not: indeed, the idea that a text can exist in complete impersonality, without a directing author, is itself ideological, trying to cast Art as something timeless, not constrained by history, or produced in definite historical circumstances. We have seen in *The Wings of the Dove* that there are strong value-judgements running through it which do interpellate the reader into the discourse of Henry James, in spite of the absence of direct 'telling'. The author's ideology is present in indirect free discourse and the interior monologue, even though these appear to make the scene more objectively presented, and open to the reader's interpretation.

Go back to the last line of 'Borges and I': 'I do not know which of the two is writing this page'. Can we try giving an answer? In context with the line before, the writer must be either the 'I' speaking in the narrative, or 'oblivion' or 'the other'. (It may be one of the two of them: oblivion or the other who writes: perhaps 'I' counts himself out completely.) Oblivion – forgetfulness – suggests to me the whole realm of the unconscious, the space where decisions are made without any conscious process of thought, without any prior awareness. Following Althusser's sense of ideology as the unconscious assumptions of a society, the realm of oblivion, where automatic thinking takes place, is just the space of ideology.

Whoever the 'other' is – the 'Borges' that has come into existence and who is taking over the 'I' perhaps – the line registers that the author is not in charge of his material – it comes from sources 'other' than him. That, it seems to me, is the real objection to talk about 'the author'. For the unique genius who writes must be replaced as a concept by the thought that more unconscious discourses, to which the writer is oblivious, shape the material, and the possibilities of what can be said in a particular text. The independent author concept must give way to the recognition that the Unconscious of a society – its ideology – constructs a text which may be 'other' to the actual writer.

For the philosopher Michel Foucault, himself influenced by Borges, the name for 'ideology' is 'discourse', and in the essay 'What is an Author?' (1969) he looks forward to the time when there will be in criticism 'no longer the tiresome repetitions'

> 'Who is the real author?'
> 'Have we proof of his authenticity and originality?'
> 'What has he revealed of his most profound self in his language?'

– but instead, new questions, such as:

> 'What are the modes of existence of this discourse?'
> 'Where does it come from; how is it circulated; who controls it?'
> 'What placements are determined for possible subjects?'
> 'Who can fulfil these diverse functions of the subject?'

These questions are difficult. The word 'discourse' appears here to describe the text as well as the ideology that subtends the text. **Can you put these questions into your own words?** As a hint, the word 'placement' suggests the role given to the person reading who has been interpellated by this discourse.[6]

DISCUSSION

1   The first question asks for a consideration of such matters as why a particular text assumes one form or another – television, or novel, for instance – if a novel, what publisher, and if television, what kind of audience? The genre of the discourse sets up rules for existence; what are these, and why has there been the choice of that particular mode of expression?

2   What particular discourse or ideology has produced the text? The question requires an inspection of what in the moment of history has allowed the text to appear. Further, what keeps it in existence? And why? Why are some narratives given more status than others? (E.g. the novels that get on the Booker Prize shortlist: what non-literary factors operate here? Or what explains the 1980s' interest in soap-operas and police-series?)

3   The question asks how the narrative interpellates the reader; what positions it allows the reader to adopt. (Certain types of opposition to particular controversies are allowable, but others are not catered for.) It also suggests that the narrative creates the actual 'author' as subject – as happens to 'Borges' in 'Borges and I'. Dickens's desire to hold on to his readers in *A Christmas Carol* may reflect his anxiety to preserve himself as the popular author of his earlier fiction, with the reputation that that had given him.

4   Here the issue turns on the 'author', who cannot possibly be aware of all the determinants – belonging to the ideology and modes of discourse of a society – that operate to produce the text the way it is. Half of the text belongs to oblivion – to factors the writer can only be unconscious of. The idea of the single author, someone who can be written about as 'Borges' or 'Dickens' or 'George Eliot' obscures the issue. Foucault invites us to look at texts as a mesh of different discourses at work within the ideology of a society, and producing contradictory, non-unified texts with many centres. Feminist criticism would add that discourse is bound to affect male and female subjects differently: to this extent, it is important to remember that the voice that speaks is gendered.

Appendix: Does the Narrator Matter?

In Chapter 3 I argued that the narrator has no more status than any other character in a text: and it really makes no difference whether a text is narrated by an 'I' or is told in the third person. Both Jane Eyre and the narrator who appears in *Tom Jones* are fictional creations: it would be a fiction to say about either of them that they were omniscient. So why spend time on a dead issue?

But it seems relevant to note the different ways the fiction of a narrator is employed in texts, for it brings us up against the various rhetorical strategies by which a narrative interpellates the reader. The fiction of the narrator sets up a specific way of reading the text, the author's preferred way for us. Thus I would like to follow Genette's categories a little further.

He distinguishes, you recall, between narrative that is non- or zero-focalized, and that which is focalized. In the first category comes *A Christmas Carol* or 'Fanny and Annie'. In the second, comes *The Wings of the Dove* or 'Borges and I', or *Jane Eyre*. These are internally focalized, but Genette also has in mind externally-focalized narration, where plainly the narrative holds back from stating everything. We get actions, for example, but no explanations – a typical move in detective fiction.

In the category of internally-focalized narrative, the question to be asked is 'Who is the character whose point of view orients the narrative perspective?' (*Narrative Discourse*, p. 186). The point of view dictates the *mood* of the piece. Attention to focalized narrative also impels attention to the *voice* – who is speaking? Whose attitudes are we listening to, besides hearing the story they tell? On the basis of these distinctions, Genette finds four patterns to illustrate the status of the narrator. These are based on two issues: narrative level and degree of participation.

The first concerns the status of the narrator: a first-degree narrator gives the dominant narrative, a second-degree one does not (extra- or intra-diegetic). An extradiegetic narrator stands outside the text given.

Secondly, is the narrator involved in the story or not (homo- or heterodiegetic)?

Using this classification, we have the four following distinctions:

1 Extradiegetic/heterodiegetic: here the first-degree narrator speaks, but is absent from the story. Homer and Virgil, as epic writers, provide examples. So also 'Fielding' as he narrates in *Tom Jones*.
2 Extradiegetic/homodiegetic: here the narrator tells his own story (Genette's example is Richard Hannay's narration in John Buchan's *The Thirty-Nine Steps*); or *Jane Eyre*; or 'Borges and I'.
3 Intradiegetic/heterodiegetic: Genette instances *Scheherezade*, where a narrator tells stories she is absent from. She is a second-degree narrator, created by the first narrator, who describes her.
4 Intradiegetic/homodiegetic: Genette instances here Books IX–XII of the *Odyssey*, where Odysseus tells stories about himself. But he is not the prime narrator: as a whole the *Odyssey* is 'extradiegetic/heterodiegetic'. Marlow in *Heart of Darkness* is another example. He tells a story about himself, but the whole is given by another, anonymous narrator.

Both the 'intradiegetic' categories refer to narratives embedded within narratives; stories within stories. Examples will be found in

Chaucer's *The Canterbury Tales* (where pilgrims narrate stories
they are not part of) or the stories-within-stories that mark off
Don Quixote, or *Tom Jones* or *Pickwick Papers*.

These distinctions are highly complicated, and you may well
find scepticism about them growing as you work through them.
Are the distinctions sustainable? Are they worth making?

DISCUSSION

The two extradiegetic categories seem valid, but there seem to me
problems with the intradiegetic ones. Is (1) any more than an
instance of (2) with the addition of other narrational framing
voices that give it a context? Further, in the case of (3) isn't it a
value judgement to suggest that a narrator does not participate in
the narrative? Doesn't it depend on a particular way of reading
that chooses to put the emphasis in one place and not in another?

And is the narrator ever in a heterodiegetic position? Couldn't
we argue that the willingness to see the narrator outside the text
actually draws a false frame around the narrative? And that the
narrator therefore is always a part of the total narrative – however subordinated? Even the subordination, as an absence of the
narrator's voice, would belong to the ideology constructing the
text (absence of comment being also a marker of the way a society
thinks about events it describes). The fact that a narrative is being
given is actually part of a fuller narrative which should be the
object of the critic's attention.

I have reservations about Genette's wish to inspect questions
of internally-focalized narration under the headings of mood and
voice. They may be excellent rubrics with which to start thinking
about a text, but they presuppose ultimately that we know how to
read the text, that we understand it and know where the narrative
is going. There is a residual scientific ideology at work in Genette
that makes him propose finding such certain centres of attention
in a narrative. The narrator concept imprisons the text by imposing
a way of reading, and thus a way of 'taking' the material. It
'centres' the reading, to recall a term used in discussing 'Fanny
and Annie'. If we regard the narrator as a fiction within and
produced by the text itself, then, of course, we eliminate the
question of whether drama can be narrative: of course it is. It
might be better to drop the term 'the narrator' altogether, and
instead speak of 'the narration'.

With these provisos, I think Genette's distinctions useful, if
only because they open up for consideration the number of ways

in which a narrative is presented. But do they account for differing historical and ideological positionings which make up the massive differences between narrative texts?[7]

5. Narrative Plots: 'Character' and 'Action'

Now that we have asked who speaks in a narrative, it is time to begin on the question of narrative contents – the plot. I want to start on this with Aristotle, whose *Poetics* has had a decisive influence on thinking about the plot. The passage quoted here from the most famous chapter of the *Poetics*, dealing with tragedy, is not at all self-explanatory, but you might try working out what Aristotle means by *action*, *character* and *plot*. How do the first and the third contrast with each other, for example? The opening comments made on 'Fanny and Annie' may help.

> In tragedy it is action that is imitated, and this action is brought about by agents who necessarily display certain distinctive qualities both of character and of thought, according to which we also define the nature of the actions. Thought and character are, then, the two natural causes of actions, and it is on them that all men depend for success or failure. The representation of the action is the plot of the tragedy; for the ordered arrangement of the incidents is what I mean by plot. Character, on the other hand, is that which enables us to define the nature of the participants . . .
>
> (Aristotle: *Poetics*, Ch. 6)

DISCUSSION

My breakdown of these terms runs like this:

Action (*praxis*) 'What happens': the term has a specialized sense. To follow some of Aristotle's commentators: 'the praxis that art seeks to reproduce is mainly a psychic energy working outwards' (S.H. Butcher); praxis is 'the focus or movement of the psyche towards what seems good to it at the moment' (Francis Fergusson); 'an action is an activity designed to bring about an "end" and it has in it both an element of trained desire and an intellectual element' (Colin Hardie).[1]

Action then in Aristotle's sense is likely to be single; there will be no sub-plots. In Chapter 8, Aristotle speaks of a 'single unified action'. To give an example of how influential this stress on unity has been, take Matthew Arnold's criticisms of *Anna Karenina* in 1887:

> There are many characters in *Anna Karenina* – too many if we look in it for a work of art in which the action shall be vigorously one, and to that one action everything shall converge. There are even two main actions extending throughout the book....[2]

Character (*ethos*): as the Greek word suggests, the concept of character in Aristotle is strongly ethical. Character can only be revealed in action: if it is not manifested in some outward way, there can be no character. According to Stephen Halliwell, 'character is a specific moral factor in relation to action, not a vague or pervasive notion equivalent to modern ideas of personality or individuality – least of all to individuality, since *ethos* is a matter of generic qualities (virtues and vices) (p. 151). Later in Chapter 6, Aristotle says, 'Character is that which reveals personal choice' (*proairesis* – which has to do with moral purpose, with an act of will which starts a movement or an action, and which reveals ethical character. The word appeared on p. 19 for Barthes's action code).

Agents, performers of an action, then, show by what they do distinctive qualitites of *ethos* – i.e. morality, and *dianoia* ('thought') – i.e. intellectual perception.

Plot (*muthos* – cp. myth): in Plato, a *muthos* is a story or fable embodying a series of propositions about the world. So also with Aristotle, but he also means by it the organized nature of the story in the poem or play: hence Halliwell translates the word as 'plot-structure' and takes it and action as synonyms, since for Aristotle, the action is 'a coherent and meaningful order, a pattern which supervenes ... and arises out of the combination of purposive individual actions' (p. 143).

The double meaning of plot here compares with E.M. Forster's distinction between story and plot. Common to the analysis I have just given, and to Forster, is the sense that the arrangement of events ('what happens'), their pattern, or structure, is what makes an action into a plot.

A model for plot would be Sophocles' *Oedipus Tyrannus* (429 BC). Oedipus was King of Thebes and his wife was Jocasta. But despite being the hero who had answered the Sphinx's riddle – 'what goes on four legs in the morning, two legs in the afternoon and three legs in the evening' – with the solution 'Man', which lifted Thebes from the plague the Sphinx had imposed – he did not know that the man he had killed many years before at a crossroads had been his own father Laius, and the woman he had married was his mother. The play shows his discovery of these truths. At its start, there is a pestilence afflicting Thebes. In the play's Prologue, Oedipus is told by the Priest that this can only be relieved when the murderer of Laius is discovered. Oedipus resolves to discover who the murderer is. In the first scene, or 'episode' of the play, the blind prophet Tiresias tells him that he is the murderer, but he refuses to accept this, mainly because he repudiates Tiresias' means of knowledge, his non-scientific use of haruspication, unlike his own rational knowledge, which had destroyed the Sphinx. But by the end of the fourth episode, the Shepherd appears who many years before had been ordered to take a baby and kill it, because its father, King Laius, had been warned in prophecy that the child would kill him. The Shepherd says he had not destroyed the child: soft-hearted, he had merely pierced its feet and left it to die. It had been found by the King of Corinth's servant, and the King brought up Oedipus as his own, so he never knew who his real father was. In the play's Epilogue, Oedipus blinds himself and Jocasta hangs herself. Oedipus and his children leave Thebes for ever. Oedipus blinding himself puts him on the same level as Tiresias, whose knowledge he had despised.

Now the play has already organized the action, which begins, historically speaking, with Laius being warned that his child will kill him, and ends with Oedipus leaving Thebes. It becomes a plot which works in reverse, starting near the end of the action, and showing Oedipus, like a detective, piecing together the bits of action. For Aristotle, this procedure is basic to tragedy, since it allows for the demonstration of two principles: a fundamental 'discovery' (*anagnorisis*) which the play makes and a 'reversal' (*peripeteia*) of fortune. Further, the plot-structure is marked by irony: a character goes along with information for a long time, not realizing the full import, (or the double meaning) of the knowledge s/he possesses. Literary criticism under Aristotle's influence frequently reads texts in terms of what the character – King Lear, or Emma, or Pip in *Great Expectations* – has learned during the course of the action. A.C. Bradley in his influential *Shakespearian Tragedy* (1904) locates Shakespeare's 'main interest' in 'action issuing from character or in character issuing in action' (Macmillan, 1950, p. 12).

You should be able to see these three elements at work in *Oedipus*. But, in any case, go back to the discussions of Aristotle in Chapter 2, and to the concept of mimesis as Aristotle understood it, in Chapter 3. **Using the example of *Oedipus*, what characteristics seem important in Aristotle's sense of plot, character and action?**

DISCUSSION

My list includes the following:

1 A belief in a single, firm action which presses towards an end.
2 The importance of a beginning, middle, and end. In drama, this is realized by the prologue and epilogue, with the episodes in between. When the end is reached, the problem posed at the start has been solved. This gives a 'closure' (see p. 18).[3] Thus the standard requirement of a work is its ending: in *Oedipus* the ending coincides with the culmination of learning, the discovery of the truth and its implications. In the next chapter, I shall say much more about endings, but for now we could note that a text without an ending is often regarded as a problem. Yet this seems strange. Life presents us with no endings: not even our own (we know nothing about our death). Why should we not regard texts that think they can end as problems? Are not endings – marriage, heroic self-sacrifice, suicide, a decision to believe in God or in universal destruction – things most likely to show up the cultural expectations of the society the text comes from?
3 A realistic representation (mimesis) of events. The action is continuous; the audience does not have to imagine that any gaps in time have taken place during the action, nor does the scene shift. Western criticism almost unfailingly regards it as an asset in literature to note its realism, its truth to life as it is – its sense of naturalistic detail, how people 'really' talk to each other, for instance.
4 The sense of an interrelationship between character – what people think and do – and what happens. Oedipus prides himself

on his ability to know, logically, analytically – hence his contempt for Tiresias. But he does not know: ironically he refers to himself as 'ignorant Oedipus' (line 397),[4] which may imply that his tragedy is that he depends too much on his sense of logic, which is revealed by the drama to be inadequate.

5   The stress on characters learning, moving out of ignorance, as Oedipus or Jocasta. The closure accompanies, therefore, a sense of enlightenment, of people discovering the truth about themselves – fitting Aristotle's stress on the ethical nature of drama. Critical discussion of Oedipus often centres round, for instance, questions of the hero's guilt or innocence, and on his dilemma as guilty-though-innocent. This is where discussion of character, bound up as it is with issues of free will and responsibility versus determinism (a nineteenth-century argument, especially) becomes strongly ideological. Narratives take the form of showing character developing, and learning to master actions rather than letting actions control them. A strong enough character can always take charge of his or her own destiny, and life consists of either heroes or villains.

A question for this *Guide* is whether we can think in different terms from Aristotle's? The examples that follow here interrogate concepts of character and action. We can begin with a revision of Aristotle which still keeps within his terms – Henry James's essay 'The Art of Fiction' (1884). He dismisses attempts to divide up novels into episodes illustrating character, or giving incident:

> I cannot imagine composition existing in a series of blocks, nor conceive, in any novel worth discussing at all, of a passage of description that is not in its intention narrative, a passage of dialogue that is not in its intention descriptive . . . a novel is a living thing, all one and continuous . . . What is character but the determination of incident? What is incident but the illustration of character? What is either a picture or a novel that is *not* of character? What else do we seek in it and find in it? It is an incident for a woman to stand up with her hand resting on a table and look at you in a certain way; or if it be not an incident I think it will be hard to say what it is. At the same time it is an expression of character.
>
> (*The Critical Muse*, ed. Roger Gard (Harmondsworth: Penguin, 1987) pp. 196–7)

Go back to the opening of *The Wings of the Dove* (p. 43) and to the discussion of Aristotelian narrative. Keeping the novel as a background to James's comments, could you see him as Aristotelian? How is he not Aristotelian?

DISCUSSION

1   The Aristotelian emphases here are evident in the stress on
unity and character and action – 'incident'.
2   James conceives action in a way Aristotle could not have done,
broadening its scope and giving it a psychological depth. Similarly,
D.H. Lawrence in the early 1900s thought 'George Eliot [had]
started it all . . . putting all the action on the inside. Before . . . with
Fielding and the others, it had been on the outside'.[5] Common to
James and Lawrence is a debate about character and action,
assuming the terms, and restating Aristotle's issues, which have
hardly been departed from.
      Aristotle and James do not mean the same thing by character
or by action: James is trying to push back the frontiers of definition
of 'action' or 'incident'. In *Middlemarch*, George Eliot sees
character as 'a process and an unfolding' (Chapter 15); 'incident'
is definable, for Eliot and James, in terms of the inner display of
character, as much as the outer. In Aristotle, character is much
simpler and fixed.
3   *The Wings of the Dove*, by not using the authority of a final
external narrator but in giving the movement of Kate Croy's
thoughts is closer to Aristotle's mimesis than to diegesis – so long
as we accept that any representation will be in accord with the
very conditions of seeing and understanding existing as a discourse in the society, not absolute ways of seeing and representing
reality.

**Take James's comments in relation to the opening of *The Wings
of the Dove*. How does it create character and incident? Does it
make these categories into problems? Keep the previous discussion
of the passage in mind.**

DISCUSSION

A first point might be to note the passage's length. It dramatizes
non-action (non-incident) – waiting for somebody. It redefines
incident by its very nature. In fact, the passage asks why she waits.
What keeps her? We get 'she remained' (sentence 2) and 'If she
continued to wait' (sentence 7), which suggests a moment of
self-justification, or of self-dramatization. Look at the parallelism
between the first and the second sentences:

> she waited . . . pale with the irritation that had brought her to the
> point of going away [1]
> it was at this point . . . that she remained [2]

Do you notice a slippage of meaning here? She is at the point of going away: a thoroughly English idiom ('I was just on the point of saying what I thought, when . . .'), but in sentence 2, the 'point' is her worked-up state of irritation. She remains not only in the room, but, more to the point, angry. 'Remained' is not a synonym for 'waited in' (sentence 1).

This suggests a split in Kate Croy's motivations. In sentence 1, the inversion (not 'Kate Croy waited' but ' she waited, Kate Croy') not only gives an emphasis to the name and character, but may also question the character's identity. She is 'she' before she has a name. It is, you notice, the same construction as the start of 'Borges and I' – 'It is to the other, to Borges, that things occur'. The awkwardness of construction in both cases suggests that identity is not at one (identical with) existence. Thus 'there were moments at which she showed herself, in the glass over the mantel, a face positively pale with the irritation that had brought her to the point of going away . . .'. In the light of our previous discussion, you may wonder whether she is imagining herself speaking to someone else (as in 'There are moments when I feel so angry . . .'); the poise (the 'point' indeed of 'positively pale') also seems to me self-dramatization. Kate Croy looks in the mirror not accidentally, but deliberately, to create a personality; to 'show herself'.[6] Incident here produces character, and character appears to be self-definition, finding an identity. She could not go away without losing something of her worked-up identity. In some way, sentence 7 seems to recognize this need to stay.

We have thus an interesting division. Incident is non-incident, but character is non-character. It is not just that 'Kate Croy is a self-willed person': that would be a nineteenth-century way of putting it, taking character in 'essentialist' terms (i.e. as fixed, unchanging, because part of a person's nature, which cannot be altered). James's approach to character here begins to destroy this essentialist sense of it, and of its autonomy. Character is a fiction which has to be preserved/made up through mirrors and through imaginary conversations with an 'other' – note how in sentence 5 we change to 'one' – Kate Croy is confident enough of herself, momentarily, to generalize with reference to an ideal other. This self-presentation of her mind permits for the dramatizing of her movements round the room – themselves presented in a theatrical style. But the movements add up to nothing.

It seems there are elements in James which break down the Aristotelian pattern. In that sense, he is a Modernist. The collapse of the Aristotelian slots of character and action here are most fully demonstrated in 'Borges and I'. Notice that the speaker there hardly recognizes himself through any of the mirrors offered to him – in the names on the ballot sheet, or in the biographical dictionary, or in the books that have been written. But I leave you to look back at that piece to see how my analysis of James fits there.

Character and the Subject

The idea of 'character as non-character' and 'incident as non-incident' might be investigated further, by looking at an early text. In Chaucer's *The General Prologue to the Canterbury Tales* (*c*.1390–1400), the narrator, normally taken as a comic self-dramatization of Chaucer, records his pilgrimage to Canterbury with other pilgrims whom he lists and describes: here is the beginning of his account of the Monk. In reading it you will find it easier than it looks: read it out loud, taking the spelling as phonetic and ignore what looks difficult:

```
A Monk ther was, a fair for the maistrie      [surpassing all others]
An outridere, that lovede venerie      [hunting]
A manly man, to been an abbot able.
Ful many a deyntee hors hadde he in stable
And whan he rood, men myghte his brydel heere
Gynglen in a whistlynge wynd als cleere
And eek as loude as dooth the chapel belle.      [also]
Ther as this lord was kepere of the celle,
The reule of seint Maure or of seint Beneit      [Benedict]
By cause that it was old and somdel streit
This ilke Monk leet old thynges pace      [same; pass]
And heeld after the newe world the space.
He yaf nat of that text a pulled hen      [gave; plucked]
That seith that hunters ben nat hooly men,
Ne that a monk, whan he is recchelees      [reckless]
Is likned til a fissh that is waterlees, –
That is to seyn, a monk out of his cloystre.
But thilke text heeld he nat worth an oystre;      [that]
And I seyde his opinion was good.
What sholde he studie and make hymselven wood      [mad]
Upon a book in cloystre alwey to poure,
Or swynken with his handes, and laboure,      [work]
As Austyn bit? How shal the world be served?
                                        [Augustine; bade]
Lat Austyn have his swynk to him reserved!
Therfore he was a prikasour aright...      [hunter on horseback]
```

(*The General Prologue, The Works of Geoffrey Chaucer*,
ed. F.N. Robinson, ll.165–89)

Hunting in the Bible, one of Chaucer's sources, is a godless activity; think of Nimrod or Esau. There seems room for questioning what the Monk hunts – animals or women ('venerie' and 'prikasour' are both *double entendres*). The monk whose duty as an 'outridere' is to look after the estates of the monastery he belongs to, is the object of a narration which aims to assign identity and order to differing character-types.

Dryden in the preface to his *Fables* (1700) commented on 'God's plenty' to be found in those figures, 'their general characters are still remaining in mankind, and even in England, though they are called by other names than those of Monks and Friars and Canons and Lady Abbesses, and Nuns, for mankind is ever the same, and nothing lost out of Nature, though everything is altered'. In western literature people have been thought of as 'types', subsumed under generalized categories of virtues and vices (as in medieval literature), or characterized with allegorical names, like Mr Bumble, or Doctor Slop or Mr Worldly Wiseman, or, especially in the nineteenth-century, thought of as individual figures with unique qualities. People are sometimes thought of in literary terms, as Falstaff, Hamlet, Tom Jones, or Elizabeth Bennett. An ideology of character works to say that people are always individual but also always the same: 'one touch of nature makes the whole world kin'. But 'Nature' itself is an ideological concept, producing the sense of character as basic, preceding history, as when people say 'human nature doesn't change'.

In contrast to this ideology of 'essential' character traits, the marks of unique individuality (but still codified in terms of literary types), post-structuralist criticism stresses not character but the *subject* and different *subject positions*. Here the stress is on the power of different ideological discourses to interpellate and pull the self into different subject positions: to 'constitute the subject'.[7] The person formed as a 'subject' is subjected, but also is made to think of himself or herself as free, individual, autonomous, the subject of their own actions – precisely the way in which narrative theory based on Aristotle encourages people to think of themselves. To quote Bradley on Shakespeare again:

> what we do feel strongly, as a tragedy advances to its close, is that the calamities and catastrophe follow inevitably from the deeds of men and that the main source of these deeds is character. The dictum that, with Shakespeare, 'character is destiny'...is the exaggeration of a vital truth.
>
> (p. 13)

Shakespeare is made to teach wholesome lessons about the importance of character-building and personal responsibility.

In the case of *The Wings of the Dove* we can see Kate Croy

in front of the mirror taking up a particular subject position
that in fact everything in her background has dictated for her
already. In 'Fanny and Annie', Fanny herself is seen in various
subject positions in the short story – as the governess, as the
person her aunt idealizes her as, as the potential daughter-in-law
of Mrs Goodall – in fact her choice is which of certain subject-
positions she is going to assume. Discourse precedes the individual
who has to learn to take his or her place within language (Lacan's
'symbolic order'): even the learning of gender difference imposes
a subject-position upon the child. To see 'character' as the product
of these 'signifying practices' of the ideological order of discourse
emphasizes that people are always constituted as subjects: already
subjects of the symbolic order which is learned with the acquiring
of language and culture.

   **How might a post-structuralist reading of Chaucer go? Could
we get past the common critical view that Chaucer, as well as
recording 'types', is a mimetic artist, rendering reality and seeing
people as individuals in their own right?**

   We could begin by noticing the dialogic nature of the writing.[8]
The Monk is engaged in a debate with the narrator, whose overt
comment is 'And I seyde his opinion was good'. Where the Monk
starts speaking is unclear; perhaps at 'He yaf nat of that text a
pulled hen' down to 'thilke text heeld he nat worth an oystre'.
Who speaks after the next line is ambiguous: it could be the
Monk resuming his discourse, given to us in reported speech
('What sholde he studie...'), or it could be the narrator backing
his own assessment. But if so, then the narrator speaks in the
language of the Monk; this is indirect free discourse. We assume
the Monk is speaking, but it could be the narrator paraphrasing
his arguments, rendering them in his voice, rather than the Monk's:
this would only increase the difficulty of assessing the Monk. To
argue this way means suspending questions as to whether the
Monk is right or wrong (he is normally taken as wrong!). Three
alternative subject positions are set up in this extract:

1   the rules of Saint Benedict, his disciple Saint Maurus, and
Augustine;
2   the Monk as a person in the cell, with plenty of animal energy;
3   the perspective of someone outside the monastic order
altogether.

   The Benedictine and Augustinian rules are presented in 'the
language of the other': either in the voice of the narrator, or in the
voice of the Monk, and since those voices are not clearly
distinguished, we lose a sense of individual character. Who says

that the rule 'was old and somdel streit'? The Monk or the narrator, or, perhaps, even more anonymously, 'everybody' says so: i.e. it's the common orthodoxy, so that the narration is not recording anyone's view especially.

But if the writing thus pluralizes points of view, two consequences follow. Firstly, the Monk if he is speaking, is not just stating a position, but trying to persuade the narrator, and perhaps himself. His language is rhetorical, 'performative'.[9] His character becomes an effect of his rhetoric (note the rhetoricity of 'pulled hen' and 'worth an oystre' and the questions which break up the lines at 'As Austyn bit'). We are less sure of his character.

Secondly, the break-up of a single viewpoint, when each statement is given in the language of the other means that the world is seen as itself dialogic; there is no agreed 'truth' as to what the Monk should be like. Anyone who tries to tell a truth, however final, definite and complete, discovers that the language used to do so is not their own, but someone else's; that the pure language of the self is riddled with the discourse of the other. There cannot be such a thing as a single subject position, then, which means that ideology cannot completely entrap the subject: different, plural discourses mean that every subject position is there to be contested, and to describe people in terms of a character is a weak rationalization.

Contrast this reading with that of the Chaucerian scholar Jill Mann who responds to the undecidable elements in the text, arguing that

> we cannot know whether [the Monk] even believes his own opinion; even less can we know what final judgment lies behind the narrator's hearty endorsement of it.... Faulty behaviour is presented from the point of view of its perpetrator, or can only be inferred from hints. And thus we have a sense of depth, of contradictory responses to the Monk, of not knowing him fully, of his having views of his own which make him step out of the frame of 'observation'. We become convinced that he does not exist simply on the level of theoretical moralizing ('what he ought to be' set against 'what he is') but on the plane of real existence.[10]

How do these views compare with the ones I have suggested?

DISCUSSION

Jill Mann, while responding in the spirit of Bakhtin to the plural possibilities of the text, nevertheless closes with a 'realist' assessment: the Monk is unknowable because human beings in 'real existence' are complex. There is a final 'truth' about the Monk, but we are unable to reach it: the implication being that it is Chaucer's greatness to present this complex response. An Aristotelian view of art is at work, accepting that art is mimetic of 'real existence' – even if we can be agnostic about the nature of that reality.

But perhaps there is no final truth concerning the Monk: the writing rather records different subject positions, from which voices are heard, and the plurality in each voice suggests that if you change the subject position, then what seemed to be a unique, individual voice articulating one point of view, ceases to exist, and can become one offering an opposite angle. And the plurality means that the concept of the 'opposite' also becomes a rationalization: an attempt to see people in terms of differing characters with 'depth' and 'views of their own': these implications of personal freedom are themselves unconsciously ideological.

Jill Mann in any case interpellates the reader into a subject-position through her use of 'we' – as though a late-twentieth-century secular reader (male or female) could have the same response as a fourteenth-century one. The ideology of character here assumes that neither human nature, nor readers, change over the centuries.

Beyond Character and Action

For an example of action which may be taken as questioning Aristotelian assumptions of beginning–middle–end, I would like to take a narrative belonging to a long poem, William Words-worth's autobiographical *The Prelude*. The section quoted is self-contained:

> There was a Boy: ye knew him well, ye cliffs
> And islands of Winander! – many a time
> At evening, when the stars had just begun
> To move along the edges of the hills,
> Rising or setting, would he stand alone
> Beneath the trees or by the glimmering lake,
> And there, with fingers interwoven, both hands
> Pressed closely palm to palm, and to his mouth
> Uplifted, he, as through an instrument,
> Blew mimic hootings to the silent owls,
> That they might answer him; and they would shout
> Across the watery vale, and shout again,
> Responsive to his call, with quivering peals,
> And long halloos and screams, and echoes loud,
> Redoubled and redoubled, concourse wild
> Of mirth and jocund din; and when it chanced
> That pauses of deep silence mocked his skill,
> Then sometimes, in that silence while he hung

Listening, a gentle shock of mild surprise
Has carried far into his heart the voice
Of mountain torrents; or the visible scene
Would enter unawares into his mind,
With all its solemn imagery, its rocks,
Its woods, and that uncertain heaven, received
Into the bosom of the steady lake.

This Boy was taken from his mates, and died
In childhood, ere he was full ten years old.
Fair are the woods, and beauteous is the spot,
The vale where he was born; the churchyard hangs
Upon a slope above the village school,
And there, along that bank, when I have passed
At evening, I believe that oftentimes
A full half hour together I have stood
Mute, looking at the grave in which he lies.

(The Prelude (1805) V. 389–422)

**Does this narrative fit the model of an Aristotelian plot? Consider
character. What stress is laid on the boy, or on the narrating 'I'?
Take action, as Aristotle defined its elements – e.g. beginning,
middle, ending, discovery, peripeteia – is there a reversal? Or
more than one? Are there here elements which do not fit with
Aristotle? What do you notice about the treatment of time here?**

DISCUSSION

1   There seems little of character either in the 'Boy' or the 'I'
narrating, who stands at the grave. No relationship is implied
between these two. Why does the man look at the grave? The
question has little meaning here, though there are parallels
between the two solitary figures: the boy's silence; the man's
'muteness'.

2   The first four words give both beginning and ending: 'There
was a Boy'. But what might be considered a conventional ending –
the boy's death – is not presented as an end, though it certainly
marks a peripeteia. Instead, there are seven lines following which
suggest a continuity of time: note the present tenses of 'are', 'is',
'hangs', for instance, which seem to diminish the sense of death.
The adult narrator may speak of what he has done in the perfect
tense – 'I have passed', 'I have stood', but the bank remains for
present observation, and the verb in 'the grave in which he lies' is
in the present tense – the phrase is not 'the grave in which he lay'.

3   There seems more than one peripeteia here. The boy's death is
prefaced by the silence of the owls, on some occasions when he
blew mimic hootings.

It is tempting to take the silence of the owls as prelusive to the silence of death. In which case, even the muteness of the narrator at the end might also be regarded as another peripeteia. He is reduced to quietness by the grave, pausing 'a long half hour together'. What does 'mute' suggest? Mourning – a mute? Struck dumb? Reduced to a position of being unable to write verse? Neither boy, nor Nature, nor man can produce a sound. The American critic Paul de Man connects the word with 'mutilation', as though investing the word with the idea of profound loss of part of the self. Identity is taken away by the change that has taken place (the Latin verb *mutare* means to change).[11]

We could see a characteristic feature of the narrative as action followed by a pause:

THE BOY'S ACTIVITY: Mimic hootings followed by 'pauses of deep silence'.
THE BOY'S LIFE: His life, followed by 'was taken from his mates, and died/In childhood, ere he was full ten years old'.
THE NARRATOR: Passing, but reduced to being 'mute'.

An action which is thus broken off in each case seems to cut away at the sense of life having a smooth linear development, an Aristotelian narrative. The boy's activity fits into the pattern of his life, and the narrator's also fits the pattern of the whole poem. 'There was a boy' – the beginning – that is the past tense, but the verb implies the boy's activity. 'He lies' – the ending – is the present tense, which should connote immediacy, nearness, but actually suggests total passivity. These repeated patterns form a *mise-en-abîme* – i.e. one action is placed inside another larger one of the same pattern, which in its turn may fit in another.

Action turns into passivity. The boy's hootings, which imply his attempt to control something, turn into passivity. What happens to him takes place 'unawares', as the 'visible scene' enters into his mind. There is a further *mise-en-abîme* as the total scene which includes sky and lake is further spoken of, as 'that uncertain heaven, received/Into the bosom of the steady lake'. The moving clouds (active) are held, as in a mirror by the lake, which is 'steady' (passive). And both are held in the boy's mind. In a further *mise-en-abîme* when the boy dies, he is received into the earth. Does the passage take away from the solidity of action by suggesting that activity is uncertain – hootings are not always responded to; life is cut short by death; change – mutation – seems basic – and passivity is 'steady'?

But note how the passage is built up on echoes. The owls echo the boy: the boy's hootings are mimic, echoing previously heard owl-hootings. The mirroring effect in the water is a form of echo; the device of *mise-en-abîme* is another form of echo; you can find words echoed, too, as hung/hangs; deep silence/silence; There was a Boy/This Boy was taken. Or ideas are echoed, as when 'the voice of mountain torrents' (appealing to the ear) is followed by 'the visible scene' (appealing to the eye). Does this also suggest that the man is an echo of the boy? Character changes its aspect, swung round not from Aristotelian self-discovery to further action, but reduced to muteness. It also exists only in relation to something or someone else, to which it acts as an echo. All confidences about definite character seem to me to be taken away.

This chapter has suggested the following things:

1 The dominant characteristics of Aristotelian views of narrative, and especially the part played in them by the elements of character and action.
2 Something of the force of Aristotelian views of character and action, and their ideological force.
3 The relation between Aristotelianism and the view that narrative should follow realistic, naturalistic principles.
4 The distinction between liberal–humanist perceptions of narrative as comprising characters, and post-structuralism, which replaces this concept of 'character' with the subject, and differing subject-positions.
5 The dialogic nature of narrative.

6. Ideology and the Pleasure of the Text

So we think of and experience the world in the form of narrative. We have looked at the question of who speaks in narrative, who tells the story, and have suggested that narratives are shaped

by the dominant discourse of a society, a discourse which interpellates both writer and reader, making them a subject of that
discourse, that ideology. In the preceding chapter we thought of
the ideological content of the Aristotelian plot – the form which
structures so many western narratives.

Narratives construct ways of thinking for us – which we
accept as natural, and take for granted. They give ways of seeing
and ways of representing reality in an imaginary form; Althusser
argued that in ideology, people represent not their real conditions of existence, but an imaginary relationship. The distinction here is important. Can narratives tell the truth about real
life? If not, is that a fault basic to the nature of narrative, or do
the conditions of ideology prevent narrative being anything more
than an imaginary account of reality – a fiction, indeed?

From here to the end of the *Guide* I want to examine these
two questions more closely. But at this stage, it is worth trying
out some answers for yourself. Think in terms of examples, if
you can, perhaps ones already used. For example, with the first
question, are some narratives more truthful than others?

DISCUSSION

Can narratives tell the truth? At one level, we could agree that
some narratives are richer than others in terms of truth-content.
A Mills and Boon romance has less reality than some investigative journalism (which will, of course, be presented, in book
or television form, as a narrative). Some narratives may have
explanatory power: Freud thought that the Oedipus myth explained something about intergenerational conflict. Of course,
insofar as a narrative works by fiction, it might be thought that it
cannot tell the truth directly, but perhaps the distinction between
fact and fiction is not very useful anyhow. To explain anything,
you have to move into the area of narrativizing it, putting events
into a sequence, and representing processes (even scientific processes) in forms that can be conceptualized – and the idea of
representation means that we are already half-way to fictionalizing something, realizing that you cannot talk exactly about how
things are; you have to find a suitable form to do it in.

A problem lies in the word 'truth', as well. Mills and Boon
romances do tell a truth – about contemporary ideology, the
ideology of marriage, sexual relations, social success, class, the
role of women, for example. Perhaps no narrative fails to reveal
something – about the discourse of the society that produced

it, for instance, or about the people that read or watch it.

It is also true that 'the truth' about a society, or about reality, is always a matter of dispute. When a documentary television programme appears telling truths which have been covered up by the government, for instance, the question of what 'the truth' is becomes a matter of politics: and acceptance that such a programme is accurate may only mean it conforms to a consensus view. But the consensus is also likely to be formed through ideology – 'a consensus view of reality' is a fair definition of ideology.

It is obviously true that ideological considerations place some limitations on what can be said: for example public taste, however this is assessed, imposes conditions on utterance: even home truths have to be made palatable. But the structuring of a thought or perception as narrative itself imposes limitations, bringing in certain conditions under which narrative can exist. For instance, when discussing 'Fanny and Annie' we thought of the lure of narrative: narrative exists on the basis of certain codes (e.g. Barthes's hermeneutic code) which are designed to keep the reader reading. Any narrative works by interpellation, affirming its way of seeing things – its ideology – to be a natural and inevitable way of reading reality. Narrative is thus artificial, and its rhetorical drive is only part of what Althusser means when he speaks of ideology giving the 'imaginary relationships of individuals'. In narrative, as in ideology, the reader is placed at the centre and made to feel personally addressed. Both ideology and narrative offer individuals pleasurable images to identify with. We have seen this in the stress laid on character in narrative. Writers and critics encourage readers to identify with certain characters – and to demonize others – and to see fictional characters as people they might meet in 'real life'.

Pleasure of Identification, Pleasure in Knowing

To see how ideology functions, I want to explore the pleasure the plot, and narrative generally, evokes in the reader. Pleasure comes from such things as a good story, from comic moments, from an exciting climax, and so on, but in this chapter I consider four types of pleasure which are more elusive, though they are relevant to the immediate pleasures of the plot too. Here is an example to work with, from Fielding's *Tom Jones*. The hero, the adopted son of Squire Allworthy, loves the noble Sophia Western, on whose account he has broken his arm. He wishes to finish with the lower-class Molly Seagrim, with whom he has been having an affair, and resolves that the best way is to give Molly some money, which she no doubt needs.

> One day accordingly, when his arm was so well recovered that he could walk easily with it slung in a sash, he stole forth, at a season when the squire was engaged in his field exercises, and visited his fair one. Her mother and sisters, whom he found taking their tea, inform'd him first that Molly was not at home; but afterwards the elder sister acquainted him with a malicious smile, that she was above stairs a-bed. Tom had no objections to the situation of his mistress, and immediately ascended the ladder which led towards her bedchamber; but when he came to the top, he to his great surprize found the door fast; nor could he for some time obtain any answer from within; for Molly, as she herself afterwards informed him, was fast asleep.
>
> (Book 5, Ch. 5)

Molly lets him in, and seems upset over Tom leaving her. '"And this is your love to me, to forsake me in this manner, now you have ruined me? How often, when I have told you that all men are false and perjury alike, and grow tired of us as soon as ever they have had their wicked wills of us, how often have you sworn you would never forsake me?..."'. But, as in comic drama, which is what this scene is, it appears that she is not alone: she has been busy with the philosopher Square, who is hiding behind a rug hung up like a curtain, and is suddenly discovered 'among other female utensils'. The chapter seems to justify Tom fully in finishing with her: she is not the innocent he had supposed her to be.

Roland Barthes, in 'An introduction to the structural analysis of narratives', argues that everything in a narrative is functional, 'everything in it signifies'; 'art is without noise' (to which he adds in a note that 'this is what separates art from "life", the latter knowing only "fuzzy" or "blurred" communications'). 'Art is a system which is pure, no unit ever goes wasted' (pp. 89–90). **Assuming this point, look back over the passage. Can you comment on each sentence in turn, on the details given there, many of which do seem digressive? You will find it useful to return to Barthes's codes, discussed in Chapter 2.**

DISCUSSION

1   Note how we are introduced to a linear narrative with 'one day' (the traditional opening to start off the action code); note how the reference to the arm signifies his heroism (semic code); 'he stole forth' suggests intrigue (a narrative is begun that will have unexpected results). Allworthy seen as innocent, spending

his time with 'field exercises' (cultural code), Tom experienced. Yet Tom is also innocent of women's ways, so the chapter suggests. In the contrast between innocence and experience (the symbolic code – an ideological way of dividing the world up), despite Tom's misgivings about what to do about Molly, the chapter proves his instincts right. From the confident way the paragraph opens, we are to know that there is a discovery to be made from this incident – Molly is not innocent.

2 'Elder sister' – this draws on traditional material (as in *Cinderella*) of the eldest sister jealous of her attractive younger sister. The cultural code is at work. The conflicting stories told belong to the hermeneutic code (what is Molly doing?) – the reader, who is being led on like Tom Jones himself, is being given signs of female deception (like 'malicious smile') with the intention that he (Fielding assumes a male reader) will be lured on to expect a comic disclosure.

3 Tom's innocence (i.e. lack of suspicion) appears at the beginning; his 'great surprise' suggests the hermeneutic code (what is going on in the room?). Note the evasion of the end of the paragraph – was Molly asleep or not? The text misleads the reader, for we later discover she was not asleep. Note that the reader is positioned behind Tom's shoulder, so that we see things from his point of view and learn things as he does – we also see him in the situation, so our viewpoint is more dominant than his, though not more dominant than the narrator's. We will not be able to identify with Molly; she is the object of the look, of the novelistic gaze, we do not get what she sees. With Tom Jones, however, we are compelled by the way the text constructs him as the doer, to identify with him. There is an ideology at work here, to do with the way men and women are differently perceived in culture. I leave you to consider whether Molly's protests to Tom Jones allow for any 'dialogic' principle in the narrative, whereby the point of view is not merely the dominant male's, or whether her indignation is simply a matter of comedy in the light of what happens next.

This beginning of a narrative full of comic revelations (Molly's character, Square's hypocrisy and his essential ridiculousness, being mixed up with Molly's smalls, women's deceptiveness generally) works in terms of pleasure from the reader having surrendered to the story-teller. If everything in the narrative signifies, it does so at the level of myth. This word comes from Barthes, who argues that the various connotations attached to every aspect of a society (such as, for instance, the connotations of 'elder sister' (plain, unmarried, spiteful) exist in such a seductive and interpellative force through the power of ideology that they become myths, i.e. accepted as common-sense, ordinary ways of seeing. Myth, for Barthes, 'turns history into nature'.[1] It makes us think that things are 'natural', not the products of historical configurations, produced by the operation of definite and contingent circumstances. The intertwining of narrative with mythological connotations occurs because ideological codes and expectations are being tapped in story-telling, reinforcing a community between the teller and the reader. Telling stories is a way of reinforcing cultural identity – our place within a culture, and everyone else's.

Narratives thus encourage a set of subject identifications. There is a pleasure involved here: a comforting, sustaining pleasure. Laura Mulvey, arguing specifically about film, contends that women are forced into a set of misrecognitions through such reading.[2] Texts construct them as the objects of representation, not as subjects: in watching popular cinema, are women forced to identify with male doers? In mainstream literature, journalism, cinema and television, consensual ideological models prevail, confirming certain sexual, racial and gender codifications. Literature can be alienating to some readers who cannot make such an identification, and it can be a source of misrecognition as we identify with people who are not us, who are themselves voices of ideological positions. Recognition, and misrecognition, appeals to narcissistic fantasies, about which Lacan has had much to say in his discussion of the mirror-phase: looking in a text may be comparable to a process of self-confirmation in a mirror.

The very arrangement of incidents in a plot promotes identification. Take as an example Tolstoy's *Anna Karenina*, ii. xi and xii. The first of these chapters gives the aftermath of the adultery of the heroine, Anna, and her lover Vronsky. The adultery itself is not presented: Tolstoy passes over it, and chapter xi opens:

> That which for nearly a year had been Vronsky's sole and ex-
> clusive desire, supplanting all his former desires, that which for
> Anna had been an impossible, dreadful but all the more bewitching
> dream of happiness, had come to pass. Pale, with trembling lower
> jaw, he stood over her, entreating her to be calm, himself not
> knowing why or how.

So we pass on to the guilt felt afterwards, spoken of in foreboding (and forbidding) tones, culminating with Anna's dreams after the event – one particular 'weighed on her like a nightmare, and she woke from it filled with horror'. Chapter xii opens with the reference to Levin, the nearest approach to a hero in the novel. He is the disappointed suitor of Kitty, who has just rejected him. He returns from Moscow to his country farm, still blushing with the memory of the disgrace of his refusal, but thinking that 'time will pass and I shall become indifferent'. Over a three-month pause, he does not become indifferent.

> Meanwhile spring had come, a glorious steady spring, without the expectations and disappointments spring usually brings. It was one of those rare springs which plants, animals and man alike rejoice in. . . .
>
> Easter found snow still on the ground; but on Easter Monday a warm wind began to blow, the clouds gathered, and for three days and nights warm stormy rain poured down. On the Thursday the wind fell and a thick grey mist rose as if to hide the secret of the changes nature was carrying on. Beneath the mist the snow-waters rushed down, the ice of the river cracked and moved, and the turbid, foaming torrents flowed quicker, till on the first Sunday after Easter toward evening the mists dissolved, the clouds broke into fleecy cloudlets and dispersed, the sky cleared, and real spring was there. . . .
>
> (Tolstoy: *Anna Karenina*, trans. Aylmer Maude
> (Oxford: World's Classics, 1939) pp. 168, 171–2)

I have only quoted a small section of this description of spring, but what function might it have in the context of these two chapters? What is the agency behind the spring? Why is the importance of the season stressed?

DISCUSSION

The clue word in the passage – belonging to the 'cultural code' – is 'nature': working secretly to bring about 'the real spring' (as the chapter closes), whose advent contrasts with two other events: Levin's determination to become indifferent to Kitty and more particularly, Anna's adultery. The ideology of nature is used to check the rationalizations that Levin makes about his emotional life, and to make the adultery unnatural. The narration does not need to criticize Anna at any overt level: the juxtaposition of chapters makes the condemnation clear in the relief and pleasure generated by spring. Note how nature is tied in to religion: through the references to Easter, and to the 'three days' after: three days evoking the narrative of Biblical resurrection. It seems significant that it is on a Sunday that the real spring is manifested. The freeing of the water from the ice is narrativized to encourage comparisons with the stirring of the heart's emotions. The text encourages waiting – after false starts, the 'real spring' appears: as if to suggest that it is marked by a fullness and plenitude that rewards waiting. The reader is drawn in to the text by this realistic description. The pleasure of the text ensures that there is no identification with Anna or Vronsky: the passage lowers tension; the anxieties generated in the adultery chapter are contained, recuperated in this chapter where there is a momentary invitation to pause and make an imaginative identification, following a narrative presented like a diary.

Henry James, in a letter of May 1912, found Tolstoy form- less, like 'fluid pudding': but on the basis of this, he seems very schematic in his plotting. That does not mean he necessarily planned the contrast of incidents this way, but it indicates how the plot is constructed by an only partly-conscious ideology. James saw 'plot' as the perception of 'a set of relations, or . . . one of those situations that, by a logic of their own, immediately fall, for the fabulist [storyteller] into movement . . .' (Preface to *Portrait of a Lady*). But the internal logic that connects events is itself a part of unconscious discourses at work that make such connections seem natural, inevitable.

We can go on to relate this pleasure of identification with a second, the pleasure of knowing.

The desire to know what is happening on the other side of the door in *Tom Jones*, and what is behind the rug, where Square is hidden, suggests that the detective novel (based on the use of the hermeneutic code) may well act as a paradigm for many types of narrative, accounting for a kind of pleasure, which psycho- analysis has discussed – a pleasure in looking (scopophilia in Freud's terminology) and in knowing, not free from covert, voyeur-like pleasures, as if the novelist is the intrusive policeman who knows the truth about everybody and the truth about what happened in the past. Plots often work on that basis. Think of the way Sophocles' *Oedipus* is constructed. 'Fanny and Annie' works on the question of what Harry has been doing before the short story started. *Tom Jones* ends with the discovery of who the hero's parents really were.

Roland Barthes concludes 'The structural analysis of narra- tives' speculating on the origins of narrative, and says 'it may be significant that at the same moment (around the age of three) the little human [le petit homme] "invents" at once sentence, narrative and the Oedipus' (p. 124). Later, he writes 'If there is no longer a Father, why tell stories?'. 'The pleasure of the text is . . . an Oedipal pleasure (to denude, to know, to learn the origin and the end) if it is true that every narrative (every unveiling of the truth) is a staging of the (absent, hidden or hypostatized) father – which would explain the solidarity of narrative forms, of family structures and of prohibitions of nudity'.[3] Pleasure has its roots deep in issues of the father's intervening and intrusive authority over both the mother and the child; and in the questioning of that authority, as in *Hamlet* or *King Lear*. Milton in the *Paradise Lost* extract wants to defend God the Father against the 'disobedience' of his children.

Barthes implies that the power of narrative needs psychoanalytic exploration. Attitudes to the father and mother, and to their intercourse – the 'primal scene', as Freud called it, using a metaphor derived from dramatic narrative – are productive of fantasy and of dreams, jokes and speculations, basic material for narrative. In Barthes, the boy comes to narrative and to the Oedipal stage at the same moment. Barthes also mentions 'the sentence', for he sees the typical optimum structure of the sentence (subject–verb–object) as a little narrative in itself: the requirement to think and talk in grammatical sentences, which is, of course, basic to education and to socializing, thus sets up the requirement to think in terms of narratives – completed actions, centred on a definable event taking place (every sentence must have a finite verb in it), performed by a subject. Conceptualizing life in such micro-narrative terms is where ideology begins.

Pleasure and Anxiety: Back to the Ending

Narratives generate a certain anxiety in readers, teasing them, indeed, and heightening these tensions through digressions, and then lowering them. The book which is so thrilling that it cannot be put down obviously plays with the pleasure that anxiety produces – e.g. will Jane Eyre marry Mr Rochester? – a matter of great excitement for many 'romantic' readers. But anxiety, which is desired as much as wished away, connects with fears that the energies and dynamic tensions a narrative generates cannot be put back neatly into the box at the end, that the ideological order the text starts from will be fatally disrupted. The expectation of an ending, referred to in chapter 5 as vital for the Aristotelian plot, is that all anxiety will be quelled. Henry James amongst Modernists expressed a scepticism about endings: as in the Preface to *Roderick Hudson* (1906):

Really, universally, relations stop nowhere, and the exquisite problem of the artist is eternally but to draw, by a geometry of his own, the circle with which they shall happily *appear* to do so ... The fascination of following [the narrative] resides ... in the presumability *somewhere* of a convenient, of a visibly-appointed stopping place.

Even some realist novels have problematic endings: for example, Dickens wrote two contrasted endings for *Great Expectations* (1861). Romantic texts often described themselves as 'fragments' – e.g. Coleridge's poem 'Kubla Khan' (1798), and do not end. The word 'denouement' is itself ambiguous, for it literally means 'untying', untying the knots the plot has been tied up in. But it also implies an unravelling, where everything comes out separate, not tied up or unified into a whole. Endings, then, are themselves the source of anxiety: does an ending solve anything, does it lower tension or simply produce another form of anxiety – that everything will actually come apart?

Sartre argues that a narrative demands an ending as its condition of existence. Consider this quotation from his novel *Nausea* (1938):

> ... As if there could possibly be such things as true stories; events take place one way and we recount them the opposite way. You appear to begin at the beginning: 'It was a fine autumn evening in 1922. I was a solicitor's clerk at Marommes'. And in fact you have begun at the end. It is there, invisible and present, and it is the end which gives these few words the pomp and value of a beginning. 'I was out walking, I had left the village without noticing, I was thinking about my money troubles'.... But the end is there, transforming everything. For us, the fellow is already the hero of the story. His morose mood, his money troubles are much more precious than ours, they are all gilded by the light of future passions. And the story goes on in reverse, the moments have stopped piling up on one another in a happy-go-lucky manner, they are caught by the end of the story which attracts them and each of them in turn attracts the preceding moment: 'It was dark, the street was empty.' The sentence is tossed off casually, it seems superfluous; but we refuse to be taken in and we put it aside: it is a piece of information whose value we shall understand later on.
>
> (Penguin edn., trans. Robert Baldick (1965) pp. 62–3)

How does the end transform everything for Sartre? What point is he making about information? Is there any way in which the existence of an ending frustrates the possibilities of having a story at all? What do you make of the first sentence of the extract?

DISCUSSION

1 The passage suggests that all narrative takes place from the perspective of the ending. Story-telling takes the form of repetition – to narrate is to relive, from the standpoint of a

finished position. Think of the Ancient Mariner's narration to the wedding guest in Coleridge's poem, or Pip in *Great Expectations*, giving his autobiography. Both confessional narratives and auto-biographies must be told from a fixed position at which the subject feels s/he has arrived. Without such a present position, there can be no narrative. Clearly, such an argument would 'stabilize' the text: make it necessary to read in the light of an ending which untied all the knots.

2   Sartre's sense is that all information, all detail in narrative is relevant – because the ending gives a standpoint by which the story-teller decides which details are important and which are not. This viewpoint could be compared to Barthes saying art has no 'noise'. But if we wanted to criticize that idea, as Barthes himself did in his work from *S/Z* onwards, we could say that things only signify in art if we assume the standpoint of an ending. If we decided that the ending of a text was artificial, or false, we would then have to conclude that the directions in which the incidental details pointed were not as clear as all that.

3   From the standpoint of the ending, certain parts of the nar-rative can be dismissed as merely digressive. If we refuse the concept of the ending as a rationalization, we would have to say we did not know which were incidental details and which were central: the whole division between central/incidental details would disappear.

4   If every story is told from the perspective of the end, then every story must be fake in some way. We have all been irritated by people telling an apparently endless joke, when we knew that they could cut straight to the end, to the punch-line. The tech-nique of the joke is deceptive; keeping the listener at a dis-advantage till the end. But that applies also to the detective story, and if there, to the realist text. All story-telling is marked out by something of the lie on that basis.

Perhaps the ending needs to be taken out of its dominant position. Perhaps what we call digressions are ways of delaying closure – delaying, in fact, the demands of ideology that anxieties be arrested. In Cervantes' *Don Quixote*, Part 2 opens with the desire of the knight to get on the road again on knightly quests, after being forcibly kept at home. He wants his life to be further narrativized by Cid Hamet, who has, it seems, written the account of his adventures (i.e. Part 1) so far. His anxiety that the narrative should continue (Pt. 2, Ch. 4) is a desire to perpetuate the self through the unending story: it suggests that narrative must delay its end as a way of staving off death.

An illustration of the desire for the endless narrative comes with the story by Sancho Panza, Don Quixote's squire. The apparently interminable narration is of a shepherd with his goats trying to escape from a woman, and arriving at a river which he must cross:

> 'At last he spied a fisherman in a little boat, but so little it was, that it would carry but one man and one goat at a time. Well, for all that he called to the fisherman, and agreed with him to carry him and his three hundred goats over the water. The bargain being struck, the fisherman came with his boat, and carried over one goat; then he rowed back and fetched another goat, and after that another goat. Pray sir' quoth Sancho, 'be sure you keep a good account of how many goats the fisherman ferries over, for if you happen to miss one, my tale is at an end.... Now the landing-place on the other side was very muddy and slippery, which made the fisherman be a long while in going and coming; yet for all that he took heart of grace, and made shift to carry over one goat, then another, and then another.' 'Come,' said Don Quixote, 'we will suppose he has landed them all on the other side of the river; for as thou goest on one by one, we shall not have done these twelve months.' 'Pray let me go on in my own way,' quoth Sancho. 'How many goats are got over already?' 'Nay, how the devil can I tell!' replied Don Quixote. 'There it is!' quoth Sancho: 'did I not bid you keep count? On my word the tale is at an end, and now you may go whistle for the rest.' 'Ridiculous!' cried Don Quixote: 'pray thee is there no going on with the story unless I know exactly how many goats are wafted over?' 'No, Mary there is not!' quoth Sancho, 'for as soon as you answered that you could not tell, the rest of the story quite and clean slipped out of my head; and in truth it is a thousand pities, for it was a special one ... it is no more to be fetched to life than my dead mother.'
>
> (*Don Quixote*, trans. P. Motteaux, Pt. 1, Ch. 20)

This highly linear, realist-sounding plot is metafictional, which means it comments on the characteristics of narrative itself. **Can you identify any such characteristics? For example, why does the narrative fail to hold its audience?**

DISCUSSION

1 It draws attention to the pact between the teller and the audience, who must be willing to play the teller along to get the story at all, and not want to know the end before it is revealed. But the narrative fails to interpellate the reader: there seems no point of identification, for instance, and there is certainly no sense of the hermeneutic code at work which would encourage the pleasure of knowing something eventually.

2 The structure of the story is repetition again. But not repetition as a retelling from the standpoint of the end, as in Sartre, but a way of preventing getting to the end. But in both types of repetition, there seems to be a pleasure to be gained.

3   It suggests a relation between the end of narrative and death. Think of the importance of the image of the dead mother at the end. To end means death (as the novel ends with Don Quixote's death). The narrator is actually acting a double role: staving off death, but also inviting it, for any listener is going to stop the narrator at some point as Don Quixote does. Narrative is a game with death.

There is much of relevance to this last point in Freud's speculative essay 'Beyond the Pleasure Principle' (1920).[4] Summary of such a dense argument is impossible, but in it, Freud is interested in repetition, and in the idea of a compulsion to repeat, which he discusses in its different forms, and in the idea that repetition may serve to domesticate and reduce stimuli and anxieties which the human organism receives. Pleasure Freud seems to define as a lowering of tension, gaining mastery over experiences and stimulations that would excite and depress: the instincts which support the pleasure principle being, then, those 'whose function it is to assure that the organism shall follow its own path to death' for 'the organism wishes only to die in its own fashion'.

Freud sees a double movement at work in the psychic life. One, a drive towards death, towards an inanimate state. Another, a compulsion to repeat, to go through experiences again and again which entail a coming to terms with loss and with death itself. How these two relate to each other, and to the sexual instincts which presumably are not deathwards-oriented, Freud professes himself puzzled, and it renders the text highly self-reflexive as a result, asking about its own methods of analysis and recognizing the gap between the instincts and their language and the language available to describe or represent the instincts.

But this double movement is suggestive if we are to say that narrative, like Sancho Panza's, is constructed by a double desire – to close itself off and contain the anxieties it has raised, to 'have done with all the rest' (*Mansfield Park* – see p. 28), and by a desire to perpetuate itself through repetition. If it ended, if it reached closure, that would indeed be death, for it would mean surrendering to the pressure of ideology which shuts off all energies and desires that threaten its order and its wish – not to say its anxiety – to contain all oppositions. D.A. Miller, in *Narrative and its Discontents*[5] discusses what he calls 'the narratable' – 'the instances of disequilibrium, suspense and general insufficiency from which a given narrative appears to arise' (p. ix) and the problems of closure testifying 'to the difficulty of ridding the text of all traces of the narratable' (p. 267). What he describes here I have called anxiety: that a plot generates anxiety, which it must finally contain; the pressure for containment coming from ideology, which is itself what is most threatened and made anxious. Think of the threats to bourgeois patriarchal security offered by the adultery of Anna Karenina. Or the fear that Molly might genuinely be upset by Tom Jones leaving her – an anxiety the text releases through comedy. The ending of *Jane Eyre* is intended to solve the anxieties which that text prompts about women's sexual needs and the uncertainties that a lack of an assured class position gives rise to, and the need also to contain the sexuality of Mr Rochester. The detective in fiction has a function to contain anxiety altogether by providing the illusion that what is wrong in society is traceable to one person, e.g. Professor Moriarty, or Goldfinger. Think how every television news broadcast finishes, after a roll-call of disasters and crises, with a light touch reminding us that Britain, in spite of its anxiety-raising faults, is still delightfully individualistic, untroubled by extremism of any kind.

Viewed in that light, the concept of an ending is indeed ideological: a pretence that issues posed by 'the narratable' are capable of resolution. Or that those people who move out of the codifications of the dominant ideology under which they work – transgressive women, for example – can be recontained back in those codes at the end. The detective novel commonly characterizes those who resist codification – social deviants of all kinds – as villains.

Pleasure in the containment of anxiety relates to the pleasure of repetition, since repeating something familiarizes it, makes it safe. Narratives in the same genre repeat each other (how many people ask at the library for a book just like the romance/thriller/detective story they've just read), and a survey of headlines or of the way news stories are told registers the point that whether it is a bank raid, a hostage-taking, a royal divorce or a crisis in the government's economic policy, the same type of narrative and the same language is applicable to each: that such stories are narrativized in ways that make them familiar to each other, and reinforce our ideologically-derived sense that we know how the world is, that its issues are familiar and can be cast in forms which make its narratives already read (*déja vu* or *déja lu*). What cannot be so narrativized is in great danger of not being reported at all. Spy stories in the media look identical to the spy fictions of Len

Deighton, John le Carré and Ian Fleming. The reason for this is not that fiction copies life, but that the same narrative strategies govern the way it is possible to think about spying at all: and the conditions for the forms of such narrative are ideological.

Summary

We have thought about four kinds of narrative pleasure: that of identification, that of wanting to know, that of having anxieties quelled (hence the attraction of a definite ending), and that of repetition. These four are not exhaustive, but it follows from comments made about each of these pleasures that 'pleasure' should not simply be taken for granted: and it may well be a manipulative force, confirming misrecognitions, and thus acceptance of the positions assigned to us through the power of ideology.

7. Time and Ideology: 'The Garden of Forking Paths'

This chapter focuses on Borges' 'The Garden of Forking Paths' (1941),[1] often discussed as a story about time. I will take the importance of time as an issue inseparable from narrative, and having implications for ideology. 'The Garden of Forking Paths' is not easy, so you should begin by reading it once, and then, as a way of familiarizing yourself with it, ask these questions:

1   How many narrators has it got? Spend time rereading the first page. What type of tone or rhetorical address does each have?
2   What kind of narrative is Dr Yu Tsun's? For example, in what circumstances is it written?
3   What is it about the writing that makes it more difficult than 'Fanny and Annie'? How does it differ from that story?
4   What does the title refer to? How many things could it refer to?

DISCUSSION

1   There seem to be several narratives:
(a) In the first paragraph, an anonymous narrator cites another named narrator – the historian and soldier Liddell Hart.
(b) In the second paragraph, either the first voice continues, or another begins. It sounds like an historian – perhaps an official one.
(c) The third paragraph begins the narrative of Dr Yu Tsun, but after his second sentence, another narrator (d) cuts across him, with a footnote contradicting him, and obviously casting Dr Yu as the enemy ('an hypothesis both hateful and odd'). This narrator calls himself an editor, but editors of manuscripts are supposed to be impartial. This one is not. It may or may not be the same voice as was heard in the first two paragraphs.
2   Dr Yu's narrative is called a 'statement'. It was 'dictated, reread and signed', which makes it sound like a police confession. It is written from prison, it seems, as Yu is waiting to be hung. Is the editor the voice of the police? Does the text suggest that people who edit other people's work for Penguins, for instance, are just like policemen 'framing' someone else's narrative? At any rate, Dr Yu is not being allowed to get away with just giving his version of events. He is a demonized, marginal voice.
3   A first difference from 'Fanny and Annie' appears in the absence of a commanding narrator. We do not know how to take the events here. Yu tells a story about shooting Dr Albèrt in order to get a message to the Germans about bombing a town called Albert on the River Ancre – but all this is deliberately exaggerated and tenuous, while Lawrence's story keeps to realist detail to give it immediacy – and in fact tries to look as though it were not a literary, artificial narrative. Dr Yu's narrative looks as though it is drawing attention to the artificial nature of narrative. If it is a police confession, of course, it will be artificial and forced.
4   There should be several answers here. My list of things the title might refer to includes Ts'ui Pên's book; perhaps Dr Albert's

garden, perhaps Yu's dream of a labyrinth; perhaps Ts'ui Pên's conception of time, perhaps narrative itself, perhaps history. If it is about narrative, the text becomes *metanarrative*: narrative discussing the possibilities of narrative itself.

At this point, you should reread the text. Take note of the theme of 'time' as Dr Albert refers to it (53), and decide what is being suggested about this. Is it indeed the subject-matter of the story? Assuming for the moment that it is, it may be worth adding that one of Borges' pieces is called 'A New Refutation of Time' – an attack on the idea of time as linear, inescapable, driving on in one direction and thus compelling people to see their lives as taking place in a single direction, where everything has a cause (A) followed by an effect (B), which is unfolded by time. Notice also the 'games with time and infinity' in 'Borges and I'. **Is 'The Garden of Forking Paths' also trying to break up this idea of time, or trying to pluralize ways of thinking about it?**
　　To give my own answer to that, I will go through the piece.
　　It opens with a passage quoting Liddell Hart's *History of World War I* explaining why an artillery attack on the Germans in 1916 had to be delayed. (We are already approaching fiction, for the details given are not in Liddell Hart.) The second paragraph introduces the confession of Dr Yu Tsun, a Chinese who had taught English in the German-occupied town of Tsingtao (German 1898–1922), spying for the Germans, and now caught by the British. (Narrative is controlled by authority – by state ideology, indeed: the ideology of a country at war.) Yu Tsun's fragmented confession follows (why are the first two pages missing? Did someone get rid of them?). About to be caught by the British, anticipating his death that day, Yu Tsun wants to get the name of the town 'Albert' to his German superior in Berlin. He plans to kill Dr Stephen Albert, so that the Germans will be able to work out from the coincidence of names, the place. Borges' fiction works to break down hard separate, discrete identities: people and places take on each other's character. To get to Albert's house, he must 'take this road to [his] left and at every crossroads turn again to the left' (47) – i.e. 'the common procedure for discovering the central point of certain labyrinths'.
　　Dr Albert, whom he does not know – having taken his name out of the telephone directory (a book just waiting to be narrativized: try thinking how you could make a few stories out of linking all those names, e.g. by putting 'who begat' between each...) – turns out to be a Sinologist, living in the English Midlands in a Chinese-style house and garden, and the translator

of the novel written by Yu Tsun's ancestor Ts'ui Pên, a politician who abandoned politics 'to compose a book and a maze' (49). The book seemed a mere 'indeterminate heap of contradictory drafts' (50): Albert, however, has decided that book and maze were synonyms of each other. The labyrinth was to be 'strictly infinite' (50). He thinks of other infinite narratives, such as 'a book whose last page was identical with the first, a book which had the possibility of continuing indefinitely', as he also thinks of *The Thousand and One Nights* 'when Scheherezade . . . begins to relate word for word the story of the Thousand and One Nights, establishing the risk of coming once again to the night when she must repeat it, and thus on to infinity'. He discovered a letter of Ts'ui Pên, 'I leave to various futures (not to all) my garden of forking paths' (51). Albert has deduced that this is the name or a description of the novel, and the forking is in time, not in space.

> In all fictional works, each time a man is confronted with several alternatives, he chooses one and eliminates the others; in the fiction of Ts'ui Pên, he chooses – simultaneously – all of them. *He creates* in this way, diverse futures, diverse times which in themselves also proliferate and fork. . . . Fang, let us say, has a secret; a stranger calls at his door; Fang resolves to kill him. Naturally, there are several possible outcomes: Fang can kill the intruder, the intruder can kill Fang, they both can escape, they both can die and so forth. In the work of Ts'ui Pên, all possible outcomes occur; each one is the point of departure for other forkings. Sometimes, the paths of this labyrinth converge: for example, you arrive at this house, but in one of the possible pasts you are my enemy, in another, my friend.
>
> (51)

You should think about the implications here before reading on. It explains how in the manuscript 'in the third chapter the hero dies, in the fourth he is alive' (50). **Questions to ask: How would that kind of narrative challenge ideology? If it were possible, what would it do to a text like 'Fanny and Annie'? Does the idea of an infinite narrative connect to anything else discussed before?**

DISCUSSION

1 A narrative which combines several contradictory possibilities at once reminds us that narrative is also 'about' what it excludes. A tragic outcome could also be a comic one. It suggests there is no essential reason why characters should behave in one way only – indeed, characters cannot be thought of in essentialist terms at all, for one changed circumstance would make all the difference to them. To write a traditional narrative, there has to be a suppression – a keeping out of other possibilities. Narratives, not of the Borges' sort, are so much a part of how ideology works, for ideology always promotes the idea that its own way of seeing things is the only one.

2   If the hero can die in one chapter and be alive the next, then choices made by the writer, however natural they may seem to be, are only author's choices (decisively influenced by ideological considerations). Fanny's problem about whether to marry Harry is not hers: the problem has been set up that way by the novelist, who now tricks the reader into thinking that the problem is inevitable. There is no basic problem at all: the problem lies in the ideological positioning which the text sets up for the reader to accept as natural.

3   The idea of an infinite narrative should have reminded you of *Don Quixote* (p. 76). (James Joyce's *Finnegans Wake* (1939) would be an example of the cyclic text.) In *The Thousand and One Nights*, Scheherezade must tell stories to delay being put to death . . . here again narrative is viewed as a way of staving off death. The inability to *create*, to tell stories, is a kind of death.

These answers I have given are only possible solutions: you may feel dissatisfied with them. From now to the end of the *Guide*, I want to concentrate on these issues, so you should focus your objections closely.

But first, to finish the story. Albert goes on to map this idea of plural narratives being implicit in any one narrative, onto an argument about time:

> Your ancestor did not believe in a uniform, absolute time. He believed in an infinite series of times, in a growing, dizzying set of divergent, convergent and parallel times. This network of times which approached one another, forked, broke off, or were unaware of one another for centuries, embraces *all* possibilities of time. We do not exist in the majority of these times; in some you exist and not I; in others I, and not you; in others, both of us. In the present one . . . you have arrived at my house; in another, while crossing the garden, you found me dead, in still another, I utter these same words, but I am a mistake, a ghost.
>
> (53)

Yu says to the unsuspecting Albert, 'The future already exists' (54) and then shoots him, before being arrested by Richard Madden, an Irishman anxious to prove himself to the British secret service. Yu's words could mean, in contrast to Albert's argument, that the future is inevitable, or he could be continuing Albert's theme, suggesting that every experience contains within it every other experience – and to believe that means breaking with the concept that experiences are unavailable because of their placing in time. Albert, Yu and Madden are brought together for a moment by the labyrinth of time in a configuration which reveals their non-essentiality as characters – their possibilities of being something else. Because they are Chinese, English or Irish, they are set up in certain subject-positions which the national ideology they subscribe to assigns them: but these subject positions have nothing to do with their personalities: indeed they have no personalities, only an infinite number of possible subject-positions. The ideology of linear time – Dr Albert refers to Newton (1642–1727) as a source of this belief, and he coincides with the rise of the realist novel – sets up the belief in character as something firm and stable, not merely contingent; and of course it also helps with the continued acceptance of the pattern of the Aristotelian plot, with its beginning, middle and end.

On the basis of this, the story contains not only a discussion of time, but is also metanarrative, a theory of narrative. It is anti-narrative in its argument that all actions and events are contingent, not necessary, only possible happenings: there is no inevitability about any character or action. Further, it is obviously anti-narrative in that it tries to confound the very assumptions on which we read texts such as 'Fanny and Annie'. You cannot identify with anybody here: though it is a spy story and a parody of spy stories, you do not read it for the pleasure of 'what comes next', or for the ending. Above all, there is no sense of people's characters being fixed in a certain way, and moving through time – as 'Fanny and Annie' is precisely about Fanny's sense that time has run out for her, and she needs to make a decision now.

So what is the theory of time that Borges criticizes in this anti-narrative? Simply the sense of life going in an A–B–C–D linear pattern, an idea of time which became hegemonic in the post-Newtonian, eighteenth-century world. In such a world of time, you can see life in terms of causes producing effects: a view highly productive of narrative, if not a narrative itself. The fiction of realist narratives is that you are following the storyteller as s/he moves logically and inevitably from A to B to C, showing things happening consistently and with an accumulating sense of necessity.

At this point, go back to the argument from Sartre (p. 74). How does this support or attack the argument that narrative moves in a linear, A–B–C–D pattern?

DISCUSSION

It seems that Sartre does not accept the view that narrative goes A–B–C–D. His model for narrative is rather D–C–B–A, assuming that D is the end. Narrative pretends that it works from cause to effect: in fact it begins with a state which it calls an effect, and then tries to find an antecedent which it can dub a cause. A detective novel, for instance, is written from the end backwards. The novelist must know who the villain is first and work back from there to the original scene of the crime, but the pretence is that you go through in a logical progression. Narrative which assumes linearity is strongly ideological, buying into the concept of cause and effect, itself an ideology of empiricist science.

'The Garden of Forking Paths' contradicts time as linear progression, as if to say that there are ways of thinking about reality which differ from the positivist, 'common sense' viewpoint, which in this text is also nationalist, imperialist and war-mongering. But as an anti-narrative, does that mean that other narratives with a mimetic content, which this one argues against, are tied to an ideological perspective more completely? The question can be focused by looking at the way time is treated in narrative – for to adhere to a model of linear time and to be mimetic of it means to accept that ideology implicitly.

I shall return to 'The Garden of Forking Paths', but let us examine this question first. In discussing length of time in narrative, do we mean the time it takes to read or perform a text, or the time described within the text? We can call the first of these 'the time of the signifier', the second 'the time of the signified'.[2] Aristotle in the *Poetics* (Ch. 5) thought these two were the same in tragedy. Sophocles' tragedy *Oedipus* would be a model picture of mimetic art, because the time taken to perform it is also the amount of time the events take to happen. Actually, this is not the case, the coincidence of times is not real: the dialogue is conventional, not as it would be in real life, and it relies on a chorus to break the work up into separate episodes, and the time of the chorus does not belong to any 'natural' passage of time (there are no choruses in real life).

Taking other mimetic texts, is there a steady relation between these two times in 'Fanny and Annie', in *Tom Jones* (p. 68), in *The Wings of the Dove* (p. 43) and in Wordsworth's 'There was a Boy' (p. 62)?

DISCUSSION

Even in such a realist narrative as 'Fanny and Annie', we saw several time-scales working: fast-forwards, flashbacks, cuts, drawn-out sequences, and so on. When Fielding announces his intention to digress in *Tom Jones*, we are aware of a feature at work in nearly all story-telling: its readiness to speed up or slow down for effect.

In the passage from *The Wings of the Dove* we have a series of references to time which are appropriate in the context of Kate Croy waiting for her father: the feeling of boredom and of endless pointless movements round the room to kill time is strong, but it is significant that we are never told how long her father keeps her waiting, how long 'unconscionably' means (two minutes or half an hour?): length of time is seen as something subjectively felt, not objectively registered – in some circumstances, two minutes seems like half an hour, and in others, half an hour seems like two minutes. Different people register the lengths of time differently, so it might not be at all useful to say just how long Kate Croy had been kept waiting: some readers would sympathize with her, others would not.

With Wordsworth, there are precise time-references – 'ten years old' – 'a full half hour together'; the time of day the boy was active is specified, but the text also comes near to destroying the concept of linear time, as in the sudden change of tense of 'a gentle shock of mild surprise/Has carried . . .' – a use of the perfect tense that contradicts every other use of the past tense and which suggests that this event has happened outside any other time-scale alluded to in the text. The tense virtually contradicts the sense that the boy has now died.

It seems that each of these texts sets up its own narrative time, and none feels bound to the idea of a strict mimesis of time considered as a linear pattern, going on in a single direct line. Gerard Genette, in *Narrative Discourse*, his study of Proust's *A la Récherche du Temps Perdu* (published 1913–27), distinguishes different relationships between the time of the thing told and the time of the telling. Further, he finds numerous examples in Proust of anachronistic details, which frustrate the wish to join up the two times.

Genette sees the breakdown of relationship between narrative time and the time of the signified taking place in several ways:

1   *Through order:* Events happen in a certain order in life, but may be related in another; not necessarily in a linear beginning–middle–end sequence. Analepsis (flashback) and prolepsis – where something in the future is narrated or described as though it had happened already – characterize all fiction. Proust's narration gives 'achronies' – examples of analepsis and prolepsis where it is impossible to decide where the digression finishes; there is no clear return to the order of events described.

2 *Through varied duration:* i.e. of the time taken by the text in comparison to the time the events last. Duration varies: considerable space may be given to a momentary experience, or years may be summarized in a page. Think of the use of slow-motion in films, or fast-motion. Genette thinks on a duration-scale with, at one end summary (narrative duration less than historical), and continuing with the dramatic scene (where the two durations are nearly equal), and then narrative stasis (e.g. a description) where narrative time continues but historical time does not); finally ellipsis or paralipsis. An ellipsis is a leap forward – a break in the temporal continuity. There is zero narrative time in this case, as the event is not described, but historical time continues. In paralipsis there is no break in the reporting of historical time, but a particular event in that time-sequence is omitted. Detective stories, in their need to deceive the reader, are strong on paralipsis: omitting a vital feature while ostensibly narrating all that happened.

A narrative may pause – as in opera, where a song may simply give people's feelings, which are not separable in time from the events they have been abstracted from. The diegesis splits them up into action and comment. Narration separates modes of action that are simultaneous: thus narration tends to double historical time, and ceases to be mimesis.

3 *Through frequency:* It may be ambiguous when or how often an event occurs. There can be a 'singulative narrative' (telling once what happens once), or a 'repetitive narrative' (an obsessional telling several times of what happened once: going round the subject) or an 'iterative narrative' – where a single narrative assertion covers several occurrences of the same event, or similar events. The effect gives a sense that certain moments in life are analogous to others, and may well be thought of together, and suggests the combinatory or associative effect of memory. Thought about past events and their sequence may take place on thematic, not chronological lines. A grouping of disparate events together because of some common basis – say their geographical setting, or their personnel, or because they all happened on a certain day of the week – is a syllepsis. We may add to this category by speaking of the 'pseudo-iterative', where the story narrates as something that happened repeatedly an event the precise details of which make it obvious it only happened once.

Now this list may have taken some working through, but its idea is simple. It draws attention to the massive disproportion between an actual historical event and its place in representation. To get from the representation of an event to the actual event (to what happened) is a virtual impossibility, even where the representation pretends to follow the events almost exactly in time. Genette argues that Proust's exploiting of different times of the signifier breaks down a traditional mimesis and diegesis and subverts narrative representation altogether. The narrator, while appearing to give a single viewpoint, by using an iterative narrative destabilizes the idea of the reader receiving an account of localizable, identifiable events. Proust's work frustrates the attempt to reach from the time of the signifier to the time of the signified.

Linear Time and Ideology

What are the implications of Genette's sense of the break between these two times? The way we experience an event already narrativizes it. An event, to be registered as such, has to enter a textual, narrativized, form. Our understanding of time as linear is itself a representation, with strong ideological associations. The time of the signified is not 'natural' time: it is events represented in a certain order which we take to be natural. The time of the signifier may play out events say as C–B–A–D, instead of A–B–C–D, but *both* are representations, and both connect therefore to ideological understandings of reality. There is no original real-life time against which we can check narrative time: however you consider real-life time, you must think of it in some represented, narrative form – even a sense of time as linear is a representation of it, just as the word 'time' is an attempt to conceptualize something felt about the nature of reality.

At this point, remember Althusser's sense of ideology as that which affords a view, an 'imaginary' reading of the way things are. Althusser takes literary texts to be themselves linked to the ideology of the society producing them. Thus the critic Terry Eagleton refers to Dickens's novel *Bleak House* (1853–4), and argues that for all the use of 'realism' in the book,

> we should not be led by this to make direct comparisons between the imaginary London of his novel and the real London. The imaginary London of *Bleak House* exists as the product of a representational process which signifies not 'Victorian England' as such, but certain of Victorian England's ways of signifying itself. Fiction does not trade in imaginary history as a way of presenting real history; its 'history' is imaginary because it negotiates a particular ideological *experience* of real history.[3]

How does Eagleton counter the idea that *Bleak House* is a reflection of Victorian society? What does he see *Bleak House* as 'about'?

DISCUSSION

He argues that *Bleak House* gives a knowledge of Victorian ideology: about 'certain of Victorian England's ways of signifying itself'. The word 'signifying' could be replaced with 'representing'. The novel does not tell us so much about Victorian London as about the way Victorian London existed in ideology – it shows us how the Victorians (the dominant middle-classes) represented London and its problems to themselves. The 'history' in *Bleak House* is 'imaginary' because it fits with the preferred self-image the Victorians had, and it flatters their sense of themselves in relation to their real history.

He is not claiming that the narrative stands in a flat relation to ideology, just reflecting it passively, or acting as its voice. And while he does not use the word 'narrative', he uses another, equally important: 'history'. Immediately we think in terms of history, we are faced with issues of time. Not just the amount of time spent writing *Bleak House*, but also that the narratives – there are several – in the novel record a progress in time. The importance of narrative is that it is somehow bound to respect our perception of events – that they are themselves shaped by time and take place within time. Our sense of events cannot be static: not only do events happen in time, but so do our perceptions of them – which implies that ideology itself, as a representation of things, must take on itself the features of narrative. To represent, or to signify a state of affairs to yourself means seeing it in a sequence, as a narrative.

Thus the relationship between *Bleak House* and the dominant ideologies it relates to must be one between narratives. And to refer to ideology as a narrative comes close to destroying its homogeneity. For the condition of a narrative's existence is that it is subject to the deferring effects that are introduced as soon as we see that things do not happen, and cannot be represented as happening, in an instant. As soon as we add in the separating effects of time, we affirm difference and the impossibility of seeing things as a unity. Mimetic narratives may look as though they reflect ideology, but both narrative and ideology, as narratives, are already dispersed, not existent as a totalized static reality. Time, as that which spreads out and which when it permits repetitions ensures that they are somehow seen as different from each other (if only because they are seen as repetitions) could be regarded as the potential destroyer of the pretensions of ideology to offer a complete and satisfactory representation of how things are. It breaks up the unity of a narrative text, separating its statements out and exploiting the differences between them.

'The Garden of Forking Paths' and Ideology

An objection to what I have said thus far might run like this: it implies that ideology is not important, because narrative can show it up for what it is. In that case, what is the fuss about? Is there anything constraining the way people think about or represent reality?

Another objection might follow from an earlier discussion, where I suggested that Borges' idea of narrative suggested that in 'Fanny and Annie', Fanny's problem – should she marry Harry? – is one set up by the novelist, not actually therefore a 'real' problem. Isn't the point that Lawrence is describing a real situation, and that it is possible to see Fanny's situation – or Harry's, or Annie's – as important and actually worth identifying with?

You should decide what you feel about these points. Can you relate them back to Borges' text – or to Lawrence's?

DISCUSSION

1   It seems evident that Borges, at any rate, does not believe that narrative is free. In the story, it is the power of the police, who are significantly absent from the text, which arrests and extorts confession: narrative is a way of forcing people to choose one option or another and of persuading them that there is only one course to follow, only one set of possibilities. In other words, Yu Tsun's narrative is contained within an uncomprehending one given by an 'editor' who is in charge of 'official' history and regulates it, and who, along with the police, is the representative of what Althusser calls the 'ideological state apparatus', if not the 'repressive state apparatus'. The designation emphasizes that ideology is produced by the state and represents its interests. Narrative is induced by the forces of the state and its power, and is not free or spontaneous. However hollow ideology may actually be, its power is felt.

In fact Lawrence's and Borges' stories have this connection: both relate something real, tied down to social existence. Dr Albert discusses an alternative kind of narrative, one that would in effect cut free from state power (notice that the ancestor, Ts'ui Pên, had to leave the interests of state in order to become a writer) – but the text Dr Yu gives could well be argued to be a mimetic one, in spite of its elements of parody of the spy-story genre.

2   I have a lot of sympathy with the second objection. Nonetheless, it is worth emphasizing Eagleton's sense of a text not actually describing history – the actual conditions of social existence,

whether in Dickens's London, or in Lawrence's English Midlands – but giving ways of representing that existence – i.e. in ideology. These ways are bound to leave out significant areas of life. A dominant ideology may seem to account for all areas of social existence, but it is actually built on gaps: silences about certain problems, the inability to represent certain social groups, such as the working class in Victorian fiction, who get very short shrift on the whole, even in Dickens; or women; or certain aspects of sexuality. A text may well show up the silences and the gaps in the ideology, for instance, by the way its own explanatory force stops short, owing to its involuntary commitment to an ideological standpoint.

If this point is accepted, it follows that the text, however mimetic it may seek to be, cannot only deal with real-life problems as these are set up in ideological representations – which also, of course, propose their own range of solutions. However impelling the textual issues may appear to be, they are problems posed in a particular way – though the narrative may actually have the power to question the assumptions implicit in such a setting up.

This argument about ideology suggests that what the text does not say is as important as what it does say. Dr Albert makes the point when he says that in a riddle whose answer is chess, the only prohibited word is the word chess itself (p. 53). A text may try to speak unconsciously of things it suppresses at the directly conscious level.[4] If we accept this point, we would have to say that the subject of 'The Garden of Forking Paths' is not really time, since it discusses that quite openly. What do you think its subject may be? (A clue: note that we have already seen that the power of the police is not referred to openly.)

DISCUSSION

I can only give my own answer to the 'riddle', of course. There is an important off-stage absent narrative at work. Yu Tsun belongs to one colonized people (the Chinese in Tsingtao); Madden belongs to another (the Irish, under occupation by the British in 1916). The imperial powers themselves (Britain and Germany) are now clashing: as indeed they also were when Borges wrote 'The Garden of Forking Paths' (another example of repetition within time). What settles the destinies of Dr Albert and Yu Tsun in the story is actually not mere contingency, but the power of politics – or of ideology. If Borges wishes to suggest that all narratives are capable of reversal, he is actually reckoning without the force of history and political ideology – but interestingly, these very forces are present (though also absent: off-stage) in the text.

I leave you to consider whether the narrative I have constructed of the 'real' subject of 'The Garden of Forking Paths' – the control of agencies by imperial powers who know how to manipulate their pawns – is anti this 'anti-narrative' or not. But it fits the point that character is not essential, but brought into play through contingent circumstances. Neither Yu, Albert or Madden are acting in a way that would be expected of them. All of them occupy subject-positions which seem betrayals of their own 'natural' conditions. Just as Ts'ui Pên changed direction in his life, so all allegiances seem temporary, capable of several different inflections. This switching of allegiances can be healthy: Dr Albert went out to China as a missionary (to impose a narrative of Christianity on the Chinese) and was taken over by the Chinese discourse, so much so that he can now explain the workings of Ts'ui Pên to his descendant, Dr Yu Tsun. Chinese ideology is illuminated by somebody who stands outside that ideology: which may suggest that narratives can indeed show up some ideologies, and make people see what underlies them.

Summary

At the end of this chapter, you should:

1   Have a sense of the possibility of an anti-narrative, and know what it is contesting.
2   Be able to see why narratives need to contest the ideology of linear time.
3   Have a sense of the way narratives can contest ideology, simply by being narratives set in time.
4   Be aware of the proposition that texts are formed of absences and gaps, and of positions that they cannot articulate.

8. In Defence of Narrative

We have considered the strategies by which literary narratives work, and how they relate to the ideology producing them. Literary narratives are examples of the narratives we encounter daily, which surround us all day. In these last chapters of this *Guide*, I turn attention onto narrative itself, and to a contemporary debate which exists amongst those theorists of culture who describe the late twentieth-century as the period of 'postmodernism'. Much of the controversy over the postmodern centres on issues connected with narrative. Should it be avoided because it imposes a way of thinking? Are historians, for instance, limited by writing history as a narrative of events? Could history be written as an anti-narrative? What are the gains and losses involved in narrativizing, or not narrativizing? If it is so linked to ideology, how may that connection be broken, if at all?

Narrative simply because it tells a story is under suspicion. The poet Philip Sidney (1554–86) felt that it was important that the poet, while meaning to 'win the mind from wickedness to virtue', did so by a story. 'With a tale forsooth he cometh unto you, with a tale which holdeth children from play and old men from the chimney corner' (*Apology for Poetry*). People are often embarrassed at the idea of liking a good story. E.M. Forster's 'Oh dear, yes, the novel tells a story' reminds us how little the story-aspect of writing has been thought important enough to give attention. In Shakespeare's *Othello*, its power connects with seduction, sexuality and enchantment. As in Othello's narration in self-defence to the Venetians, speaking of his wooing of Desdemona and explaining why she has married him:

> My story being done,
> She gave me for my pains a world of sighs.

She swore in faith 'twas strange, 'twas passing strange;
'Twas pitiful, 'twas wondrous pitiful.
She wished she had not heard it; yet she wished
That heaven had made her such a man. She thanked me,
And bade me, if I had a friend that loved her,
I should but teach him how to tell my story,
And that would woo her.
                                    (*Othello* i. iii. 157–65)

Telling a story is seductive. At Desdemona's request, Othello tells his life-story, as he has told it to her father, and as he speaks, 'often did beguile her of her tears' (line 155). 'Beguile' suggests the duplicity inseparable from narrating and in a narration: you should be able by now to think of how telling stories involves deception. Othello may tell the exact truth to Desdemona, but 'beguile' implies trickery, or magic. *Othello* is full of people telling stories to each other. This story the hero tells the Venetians draws the Duke on to say 'I think this tale would win my daughter too' (line 170). Narrative lays its audience under its spell – as happens with Othello, when Iago tells him stories about Desdemona and Cassio.

In contrast to this, in *S/Z* Roland Barthes analyses Balzac's short story *Sarrasine*, where the narrator tells the story of Sarrasine to a woman as part of a contract; 'the truth in exchange for a night of love', but 'it turns out to be the story of a terrible disease animated by an irresistible contagious strength; carried by the narrative itself, this disease ends by contaminating the lovely listener and, withdrawing her from love, keeps her from honouring the contract' (pp. 212–13). The woman's final words are 'No-one will have known me'. 'Knowledge' here is clearly sexual, playing on the old Biblical meaning of 'to know' (= carnal knowledge). It is interesting that the etymology of the word 'narrate' relates to 'gnarus', knowing (cp. 'cognoscere'): narrative is a way of knowing the world.

What implications might this image of narrative as a form of seduction have? Does it make narrative more or less important? Or problematic? Consider both the narrator and the reader in your response.

DISCUSSION

1   For Barthes, the woman's refusal to take part in the denoue-ment the man has in mind for her – his plot – is akin to a refusal to let herself be narrativized, to allow anyone to make a story of her. For the implication of narrative-as-seduction is its power to

'know' a person or subject as fully as though they were sexual objects. Without such an ability, there could be no 'good story'. All this strongly suggests negative aspects of narrative.

2 If the narrative of Sarrasine has already, to quote Barthes, 'contaminated' the woman, it implies that narrative texts do have, and have had historically, immense ideological effects. If the woman allowed herself to be seduced, that would be one result, but the implication is that her refusal is equally a mark of the narrative's effect – it compels her to an isolation which is virtually a form of death. We recall, following the discussion of Don Quixote and of 'The Garden of Forking Paths', that the absence of narrative is death, that an ideal Borges holds out is of an 'infinite narrative'.

3 The conventional image of seduction suggests a male active writer/narrator and a female passive reader, who must surrender to the power of narration. Is there any way in which there can be a counter-seduction, as it were, by which the reader ceases to be passive? Can narratives be turned back on themselves? Or must narrative be refused altogether?

I have raised the debate around narrative in this abstract way, but we must now turn to specific arguments within postmodernism.

Narrative and Postmodernism

In both Modernism and Postmodernism, there has been a breakdown of belief in narrative – particularly in the grand narrative offered by the European realist novel which offered to explain everything, to incorporate everything in its scope. The Marxist literary critic Georg Lukács (1885–1971) discussed a breakdown of linear narrative in the second half of the nineteenth century in Flaubert (1821–80), and its decay into what he saw as the merely descriptive, passive Naturalism of Zola (1840–1902). Flaubert's practice proclaims narrative as empty. In a letter of 1852, he wrote, 'What seems to me ideal, what I should like to do, is to write a book about nothing, a book with no reference to anything outside itself, which would stand on its own by the inner strength of its style, just as the earth holds itself without support in space, a book which would have almost no subject, or at least where the subject should be almost imperceptible, if that were possible'. Genette associates Flaubert with a *'de-dramatization . . . almost de-novelization* of the novel with which the whole of modern literature seems to have begun' (*Figures of Literary Discourse*, p. 200). He quotes Flaubert on the ball-scene in *Madame Bovary*: 'I had to write a narration, and narrative is something I find very tiresome' (p. 202). This is symptomatic of developments in writing at the end of the nineteenth century. Joseph Conrad (1857–1924) and Ford Madox Ford (1873–1939), who wrote with him, themselves felt the absence of life as narration: 'we saw that Life did not narrate, but made impressions on brains'; 'a novel must therefore not be a narration, a report'.[1] You could add to this Virginia Woolf's objections to conventional narration, as quoted earlier (p. 7), James's comments in 'The Art of Fiction' (p. 55) and E.M. Forster's distaste for 'story'.

Lukács associated the loss of narrative with the failures of revolution in France and Europe after 1848, the 'year of revolutions', and the triumph of a reactionary, no longer revolutionary, bourgeois ideology as a result. Its failure coexists with the loss of political solutions: people cannot find a way forward out of their present discontents, and all that is left is the passive writing of naturalism (writing reduced to a photographic detailing of things as they are), or the breakdown of meaningful social action in modernism. Human lives under capitalism suffer from *reification* – they are reduced to an object-status – people's options for action in the world of advanced, global capitalism are pseudo-choices only.

But Lukács' devaluing of Naturalist and Modernist narrative is open to Brecht's satire, that according to Lukács modern writers 'just have to keep to the Old Masters [= Balzac, Scott, Goethe, Tolstoy, Thomas Mann], produce a rich life of the spirit, hold back the pace of events by a slow narrative, bring the individual back to the centre of the stage and so on'.[2] In contrast to this looking back, Brecht argues that new forms of writing have to be found simply because definitions of what is 'real' are not static: they change as shifts in ideology allow certain things to be represented, while blinding texts to other things that thereby escape representation. Definitions of what is real are political: they come about from constantly shifting ideological perspectives which mean that there never is a settled single view which everybody holds of what constitutes the real. Postmodernism, for instance, has attended to local narratives which historically have not been heard – women's stories, working-class, oral narratives, the lives of people whose ethnicity prevents their voice being articulated. An historical account focusing on women, for instance, may well be an 'anti-narrative' in working against the grain of accepted historical narrative, where it is assumed that the agents of history are men.

The postmodernist philosopher Jean-François Lyotard states:

'Simplifying to the extreme, I define *post-modernism* as incredulity towards metanarratives'.[3] What change of thinking does this register?

The nineteenth century produced many metanarratives: i.e. narratives with the power to explain other smaller narratives. For instance, Darwinism, Marxism, psychoanalysis, the belief in history and historical development – these were powerful explanatory tools in the nineteenth century to account for the situations people found themselves in, and to point the way forward out of their discontents. These narratives could be used to legitimate knowledge, to give it an authority. Lyotard argues that there has been a decline of confidence in the explanatory power of such narratives, and he insists on the illusion involved in thinking that what happens can be adequately represented by narrative. In contrast, the postmodern

> puts forward the unpresentable in presentation itself; that which denies itself the solace of good forms, the consensus of a taste which would make it possible to share collectively the nostalgia for the unattainable; that which searches for new presentations, not in order to enjoy them, but in order to impart a stronger sense of the unpresentable.
>
> (p. 81)

What aspects of narrative is Lyotard attacking? What do you take him to mean when he stresses 'the unpresentable'?

DISCUSSION

We have already agreed that ideology and narrative are both representations. Lyotard points to a crisis which he sees as always having been existent, but which is forcefully revealed in the twentieth century: a crisis of representation. He speaks about an aesthetic dimension to narrative: of 'good forms'. Narrative conventionally has to fit into categories of the aesthetically pleasing. For example, think of the perfect symmetries of plot, in *Oedipus*, or *Tom Jones*, or 'The Garden of Forking Paths'. Or consider how dramatically 'Fanny and Annie' or *The Wings of the Dove* open. Narrative, it seems, has to obey its own rules of form.

In postmodernism, the event and representation of the event have been shown to come apart; explanations cannot explain, because the very form of a narrative predetermines the types of explanation that can be given. In some ways, we already know this: a news story has to have its demonized figure; it has to be presented on television according to consensual values, which means that certain points of view, which do not fit the consensus, cannot be heard. (Notice that Lyotard refers to postmodernism as refusing consensus-taste.) An event is defined as an event if it is representable. Narratives tend to be the lives of people – think how political issues are regularly turned into personality matters in the media. If narratives turn out to deal with individuals, in what ways can they handle explanations where individuals themselves are irrelevant? (Think of how the argument in chapter 5 presented individual character as itself an ideology.)

Further, Lyotard sees grand narratives as legitimating forms of discourse, ways of thinking. The converse also holds: any society has a strong interest in declaring some ways of thinking illegitimate – simply wrong, out of court. The narratives people live by allow for certain ways of thinking, and de-permit certain others. Illegitimate ways of thinking are part of the whole history of repression existing in a society's ideology.

In the case of history, there have been strong objections to seeing it as a narrative, for instance in the work of the historian Hayden White. In his essay 'The Value of Narrativity in the Representation of Reality', he argues that where 'narrativity is present ... morality or a moralizing impulse is present too'.[4] Writing history as a narrative imposes a goal, a sense of an ending on events taken as part of an Aristotelian plot. White argues that nineteenth-century historians viewed the events of history as themselves forming a narrative structure, so that all history-writing had to do was to follow this form. But in that case, what do we mean by 'history'?

It could refer to two things: (a) events, 'what happened'; (b) narratives or accounts written by historians to tell what happened. Arthur Danto, the American philosopher, argues that history is 'a narrative structure imposed upon events'; it gives history 'followability'.[5] **How would a postmodernist object to this description of history writing? Keep the discussion of Lyotard in front of you.**

DISCUSSION

The objection would be over 'followability'. It suggests that the events of history can be adequately represented, that our present perspective can be an adequate measure to grasp events. Yet it is questionable whether history can avoid being a narrative – or a contest of narratives, of which one interprets events correctly. 'The Garden of Forking Paths' begins as a contest over which historical narrative is to be preferred, and Borges seems to suggest that such a contest is actually over different fictional representations.

The French *Annales* historians take history as a science and refuse to narrativize, because narrative would turn into a commanding Grand Narrative. History must become a science for, White argues, in the physical sciences there is no room for narrative-like explanation.

> biology became a science when it ceased to be practised as 'natural history', i.e. when scientists of organic nature ceased trying to construct the 'true story' of 'what happened' and began looking for the laws, purely causal and non-teleological, that could account for the evidence given by the fossil record, results of breeding practices, and so on. To be sure ... a *sequential* account of a set of events is not the same as a narrative account thereof ... the difference ... is the absence of any interest in teleology as an explanatory principle in the former. Any narrative account of anything whatsoever is a teleological account.
>
> (p. 217)

A teleological account moves towards one definite end, seeing events going in a certain direction, and reading from that perspective. **Do you agree with White's definition of narrative as teleological? (You may find it helpful to go back to E.M. Forster's discussion of story and plot – Chapter 1.) Does White convince you that historians – and we – should be wary of narrative? Or that they can be free of it?**

DISCUSSION

I think White is ensnared by an Aristotelian sense of narrative – he reads narrative as though there were only the Aristotelian plot, heading towards a firm closure, which allowed for moralization. I do not agree that the biology he describes necessarily escapes being narrative: if things appear in a sequence there seems to me already an implicit plot, even if it is only like Forster's 'The king died and then the queen died'. Forster did not think this was a plot, but that may be too literal-minded: the very statement asks people to find connections between the two halves of the sentence. I suspect the desire for objectivity which marks out science (this includes, of course, the desire for freedom from ideology) makes for the wish to take this scientific description as non-narrative. That itself involves an ideology (the belief in objectivity) and belongs to a whole narrative of how natural history became biology, into which narrative the explanation may be fitted. It is thus part of a narrative, even if we agreed that in itself it was not a narrative.

Perhaps, then, White is caught by the issues inherent in the

Aristotelian narrative and is suspicious of narrative because of that. We have already considered how the Aristotelian model of narrative may prove powerfully supportive of ideologies of character, and of life marked out as progress and defined through causes-and-effects which can be known and detailed, and culminating in a conclusion which is also a 'closure'. Yet the matter does not end there. Like it or not, we are all probably interpellated to some degree into such a view of plot, which is also a view of life, our own life included. Hence people like to read something which has a good story in it. As White puts it in another essay in which he discusses the work of Ricoeur, of whom later, 'a meaningful life is one that aspires to the coherency of a story with a plot. Historical agents prospectively prefigure their lives as stories with plots.' (p. 173). We noticed at the beginning of this *Guide* that this was certainly true of Othello – his suicide has to be justified to himself by a narrative that he wishes to give in his own way before he actually kills himself. In the present, those plots are bound to be imitative of the stories we read, or consume in watching, for instance, television drama. (Raymond Williams's opening essay in his book *Writing in Society* (1984) points out that 'on television ... it is normal for viewers – the substantial majority of the population – to see anything up to three hours of drama, of course drama of several different kinds, a day'.) When seeing drama has become such an habitual experience – to say nothing of going to films or even to the live theatre – we can say we live in a 'dramatized society', one where experiences are already wrapped up, encoded, in fictional or representational forms. (Not all experiences, of course – only those which a society's consensus values agrees to show.)

Now this desire to see life as 'meaningful', with the coherence of a plot, is of basic importance to the defences of narrative given in Ricoeur, and Jameson, also to be discussed later. It certainly accounts for the hostility that many Modernist texts have produced – those of Henry James, Kafka and Woolf, for instance – where narrative and meaningful action seem to have ceased. Or take 'Borges and I', where the narrator seems to imply the impossibility of being able to take any personal action, as when he says 'my life is in flight and I lose everything'. The narrator here is not sure of anything, it seems, not even of his own 'coherence' as a person with his own autonomy. The same absence of a personal narrative we have noticed in Wordsworth's 'There was a boy'. Wordsworth, too, has been thought of as Modernist. Here, the being of the boy is disconfirmed, made to lose its self-possession through the unexpected silence which meets him, which makes him 'hang' suspended between two kinds of reality: his own and that which is outside and other to him. The narrative contemplates the end of action, both for the boy who has died, and for the 'I' of the poem who may perhaps be his mirror, who is left mute, as though no more narrative could be given in the face of the grave.

Let us go further with White's sense of the danger within narrativized history, and what Lyotard's resistance to 'meta-narratives' means. White finishes 'The Value of Narrativity in the Representation of Reality' by suggesting that historical discourse when narrativized – incidentally, a process which he argues, tries to efface the presence of a narrator, so that the story seems 'natural' and not constructed by any form of ideology – adds 'a moralizing impulse' (p. 24). 'Could we ever narrativize without moralizing?' he asks. Think of the implications of this – perhaps they affect all story-telling. **Does the statement fit with Lyotard?**

DISCUSSION

I think it does in that Lyotard's 'incredulity towards meta-narratives' involves a hostility towards any conscious ideology that could explain fully a narrative. Lukács praised the realist nineteenth-century novel for its ability to give the 'totality', to see both the whole of society as well as its constituent parts. To find such a totality would entail finding whole explanations for a given state of society. Lyotard would reject such a belief in narrative offering a whole, both thinking that such a totality is un-achievable, and that any total explanation is unreal. This fits White's sense that narrative explanation assumes, in its ability to moralize, a superiority to the material, a position above the events which can be spoken about in closed-off terms, as though the historian were in a position of dominance.

The *Annales* historians and those influenced by them (Braudel, Le Goff, Le Roy-Ladurie, Georges Duby – and, at a more theoretical level than them, Foucault, not specifically a historian at all) reject conventional narrative on the basis that it provides the opportunity for a totalizing explanation in the form of a metanarrative. Such a narrative they see as objectionable on two counts.

Firstly – we have raised this already – because of its teleology, its assumption that events link at a causal level (whereas Foucault stresses discontinuities in history), and its sense that disparate happenings can be linked together as though they were part of the same thing. For example, the word 'love' has different meanings in texts by Chaucer, Shakespeare, Blake, Lawrence: there is no ahistorical concept of 'love' that can be appealed to behind these different usages. If we referred the word back to the Christian definitions of love, as in I Corinthians 13, we would have to historicize that usage too.

Secondly, the Grand Narrative leaves out the marginal, the oppressed, the silenced, the different – it excludes the discourses of women, of prisoners, of minority groupings (such as the racially excluded), or the mad, or the sexually transgressive, all of whom work in a non-legitimate discourse. Grand narratives silence other 'local' or buried narratives which would contradict them. We need a history that hears those other narratives.[6]

Narratives and Utopia

If postmodernism has joined with other elements of twentieth-century thinking to devalue narrative, can it – particularly in the form of the grand narrative – be defended? I want to cite two important justifications for narrative, the first from Paul Ricoeur (b. 1913) the French philosopher who has written a three-volume study on the relationships between time and narrative – especially historical narrative.[7] He argues against *Annales*-tendencies in historical writing to reject history as a narrative, or as necessary to be narrativized. He sees the making of narratives as a basic human drive, fulfilling an aesthetic need for form and structure in subjective experience and secondly indicating possibilities for future action in the world. To be able to give a narrative means to be able to visualize a future.

Narrative, therefore is teleological: it points beyond itself. But narratives can only give such a possibility if they are true (historical). In this way, Ricoeur joins with the Aristotelian arguments about plot and maintains that plot (*muthos*) which he refers to as 'emplotment' must be mimetic. 'Emplotment' he defines as 'the organization of events' (i. 34). (This word 'organization' will perhaps suggest that there is at work an aesthetic aim which activates the construction of narrative.) 'I am calling narrative', says Ricoeur, 'exactly what Aristotle calls muthos, the organization of the events' (i. 36). Emplotment and narrative are identified.

What are the implications of this? As a help in answering, would Ricoeur accept the distinction between story and plot?

DISCUSSION

He suggests that just thinking about or of an event is to organize it: to have found a way of explaining it. He would not see the story/plot distinction as useful.

But what does Ricoeur map narratives on to? The answer is,

on to the 'temporal character of human experience', the point at which our being is being in relation to time, that ' "within which" we ordinarily act' (i. 61). So Ricoeur argues that *time becomes human to the extent that it is articulated through a narrative mode, and narrative attains its full meaning when it becomes a condition of temporal existence* (i. 52, Ricoeur's emphasis). That is the nub of Ricoeur's argument.

'Time becomes human' suggests that it becomes something we can think with and through. It is not alien, not a set of 'abstract moments' (i. 63) but a means whereby the self attains some reflexivity, the power to look back and understand what has happened (this entails a narration of the past) and a way to conceptualize the present (again, this leads to narrative). But – and this is the other half of the statement – time becomes human by the power of people to tell stories. Narrative only works when it is seen as the very condition in which we live our lives in time. Even passive experiences we have involve at any one moment the characteristics of anticipation and retention. An event is experienced only in relation to something else and as though it led to something else. Anticipation means that everything we encounter is experienced as either expected or unexpected, either confirming or disconfirming our anticipations. Simply to live within time means that we are constantly narrativizing experience: giving it an organization, an emplotment.

Further, time itself is not an absolute. To think in terms of time is to create a narrative of the way life is perceived. Time, especially linear time, which we discussed in the last chapter, is itself an ideology: a way of seeing and thinking that is commanding and seems so 'natural' that it is almost dislodgeable from our minds: Ricoeur, however, wishes us to use narratives as a way of finding 'a plurality of temporal levels' (i. 84). This is exactly what Dr Albert argues for in 'The Garden of Forking Paths' – and once it is glimpsed as a possibility, then old established ideas about fixed character, for example, also disappear.

Did you notice, three paragraphs back, how Ricoeur defines narrative? It needs working out. Can you see any limitations in it from what I have described of it? Again, Lyotard may be useful in your answer. In evaluating Ricoeur's work, it seems important that he makes no mention of ideology. Does this imply a limitation in his argument?

DISCUSSION

1   He defines narrative as 'a condition of temporal existence'. We cannot escape it: we are committed to it as our mode of thought.

It follows that there can be no single narrative of anything. What I think about event A depends on my present temporal state. What I will think of it in ten years' time will be utterly different, because the event will be part of a whole different set of events that happen in time. There can be no single narrative; no giving the last word on anything. (Though Ricoeur himself, thinking about history, does take his stand on a belief in referentiality (i. x, xi, 79) and he criticizes post-structuralism for its failure to do so; he is committed to a belief in an ultimate objective reality. His own Christianity is a part of that.)

2   One limitation in his work seems to be the aestheticism noted earlier: he does seem to suggest that events take the form of well-made stories. But if what can be narrated can only be what has a formal pattern behind it, then already severe limitations have been placed upon narrative as a way of recovering the past and the present. Lyotard's objections to narrative squeezing out the unrepresentable would operate here.

3   Ricoeur's sense of the possibility of emplotment does not seem to take notice of the pressure of ideology in forming ways of thinking. Conceptions of time may well be ideological, but ideology – the way we perceive people and events – is more than time, and itself perhaps more dominant over the forms and contents of narrative than he assumes.

The most considerable plea in favour of narrative as a 'socially symbolic act' comes from the American Marxist critic Fredric Jameson, whose work also uses Ricoeur. Jameson is interested in the question of whether narrative can tell the truth about history. He is in contrast to attempts to see history as inaccessible, except in the various narratives that make up the way it is represented. Recall Terry Eagleton's sense that *Bleak House* comments on Victorian England's ideology, its way of signifying itself to itself. Jameson would disagree with this, by arguing that 'history is *not* a text, not a narrative, master or otherwise, but ... as an absent cause, it is inaccessible to us except in textual form, and ... our approach to it ... necessarily passes through its prior textualization, its narrativization in the political unconscious'.[8]

This statement, and the argument, is very difficult, so spend time looking at its terminology. At this stage, I think three points might be drawn from it:

1   History as an academic subject does not simply refer to other texts which are explained by yet other texts – but all the time open to reinterpretation – history has a referent, which Jameson takes to be inseparable from the class struggle, defined as 'the

collective struggle to wrest a realm of Freedom from a realm of Necessity' (p. 19). This unfinished struggle belongs to an 'uninterrupted narrative' (p. 20) – it has gone on without any sign of finishing yet.

2 History exists as an 'absent cause' – a term derived from Althusser, suggesting that the causal elements in 'what happened' are not discernible to the empirical eye. They cannot be probed, for instance, by the realist text which depends on the ideal of empiricism (see p. 33). They cannot be analysed in terms of the struggles of individuals. As motivating forces, they are not representable in narrative form. In short, they are the 'unrepresentable' which we discussed with Lyotard.

3 Narrative ('the central function ... of the human mind' (p. 12)) is important, not because it reveals an absent cause, but because it shows up 'the political unconscious'. Buried in each narrative text, beneath the stated meaning, is its repressed one – which gives the history of struggle, of the conflict between desire and necessity.

Jameson thus recommends a *symptomatic* reading of texts. At its simplest, this means reading, say 'Fanny and Annie' not as solving a problem – of class, of the working-class community, of men's and women's sexuality – but as part of the problem, which it perpetuates by its ideological structuring of implicitly asking questions about such matters and providing suggested answers. It further means that the text should be read for its gaps and absences: we noted these when discussing 'The Garden of Forking Paths'. In those silences and aporias are located those aspects of social existence which are repressed, driven underground by the power of history which allows them no room. For Jameson, the text takes us straight back to history, but not directly. Reading a narrative will 'restore to the surface of the text the repressed and buried reality of this fundamental history' (p. 20).

Take a simple example of omission. In the discussion of *Anna Karenina* (p. 70) we noted that Tolstoy only gives the guilt felt after Anna and Vronsky's adultery – he does not record the act itself. **Look back at this example. Can you suggest reasons why not?**

DISCUSSION

You may well answer that 'it goes without saying' that a nineteenth-century novelist could not render an account of seduction as a twentieth-century writer, say Lawrence, could. Of course that is right, and it indicates something about shifts in ideology that such a scene could now be represented.

But is it as simple as that? If we argued that Tolstoy was held back by ideology, we would then have to say that nothing in the writing which followed showed that he was questioning that discourse of puritanism – indeed, he was perpetuating it by his stress on guilt. He runs along with that ideology: he is held by it as a misrecognition of reality, or at least as one way only of seeing things.

Indeed, the inability to think about the act except in terms of a consensual attitude to its consequences proclaims it as the unrepresentable (Lyotard), a 'repressed and buried reality' (Jameson). What Tolstoy cannot talk about compels us to read the chapter symptomatically. To think what Tolstoy does not think – that is the task. What would have happened if he had tried to represent the scene? (He does not even give it a context.) Could he then have maintained the stern attitude the chapter conveys? Would not that attitude immediately have appeared as repressive?

Gaps in the text may show up the failures of ideology, as we argued in Chapter 7 – or they may show the result of history's repression. Jameson understands ideology in more than one sense: firstly with the older Marxist meaning of 'false consciousness' – the way in which the exploited misread their position, not fully recognizing that exploitation, but thinking instead of themselves as autonomous agents. Secondly, he sees it in Althusserian terms: as the unspoken assumptions, the things that 'go without saying' but which 'go better with saying' – I quote Foucault – which surround and interpellate the subject, and which are, therefore, the 'unconscious' of the textual utterance. All representations of reality are ideological, but it may be possible to distinguish between those which lead outwards to collective action, and those which only confirm the individual in lonely subject isolation.

Thus Jameson suggests that there is a complex unconscious at work in the text. The knowledge and desires that ideology drives out return, in a repressed form, in the text. But then, too, ideology may form the textual unconscious itself. For it acts as the unspoken shaping force within the text, in which case, the text reveals the ideology that subsumes it. It should be clear from this that the unconscious itself is not to be read in one way: its own content is not unproblematic – it is even ideological – as can be seen from the double sense that Jameson gives to it.

Jameson's study takes three groups of texts – realist, Naturalist, Modernist (Conrad's *Lord Jim*). The narrative he offers of the breakdown of linear narrative is akin to that of

Lukács. After Conrad he says that there is a mere step to 'the perfected poetic apparatus of high modernism' which

> represses History just as successfully as the perfected narrative apparatus of high realism did the random heterogeneity of the as yet uncentred subject. At that point, however, the political, no longer visible in the high modernist texts, any more than in the everyday world of appearance of bourgeois life, and relentlessly driven on by accumulated reification, has at last become a genuine Unconscious.
>
> (p. 280)

This argument needs to be taken slowly (as always with Jameson – but I think he deserves this attention). **What criticism does Jameson make of the realist text? What does he criticize Modernism for? What does he imply in suggesting that the political has become, in Modernism, quite unconscious?**

DISCUSSION

1 He thinks that realism imposed a single way of looking: while admiring it, he nonetheless criticizes it for its relentless assumption that it could know the truth about everybody. Realism had no room for the marginal, those not absorbed into its belief that it could show the whole.

2 He sees Modernism as the force that represses history. This is a complex charge, but it links to several factors: (a) its refusal of linear narrative, which therefore sidesteps questions of what happened, when and how and why; (b) its concentration on lonely isolated figures who do not relate to the larger world outside (Kafka's heroes, Beckett's, or the speaker in 'Borges and I'; (c) its frequent rejection of the past as a source of authority. (Modernist texts often replace history by an attention to myth.) Jameson regards these implicit or explicit rejections of history as repressive, refusing other people's lives, other people's pasts and their narratives, and called his study of Wyndham Lewis (*Fables of Aggression*) by the subtitle 'The Modernist as Fascist'.

3 He suggests that the forgetting of history is a way of repressing politics. The analysis of Lukács operates here: that global capitalism, in the name of 'rationalization' treats people merely as means to ends, and constructs people as its subjects.

These concepts are part of Jameson's plea for narrative as a way of constructing or envisaging a Utopia, for making meaning, and for carrying forward a sense of new possibilities for the future. The society that cannot narrativize has lost its ability to think its way forward out of its present discontents. That entails going back to the past and declaring that what happened in the past meant something significant, something worthwhile in the long uninterrupted narrative of history itself. Not to narrativize means neither to wish to affect the future, nor to question the oppressions and violence of the past. Jameson shares Ricoeur's sense of the importance of narrative as that which makes sense of lives in time: narrative makes temporality meaningful.

In his opposition to some aspects of postmodern culture, he further argues that the 'very function of the news media is to relegate . . . such recent historical experiences as rapidly as possible into the past. The informational function of the media would thus be to help us to forget, to serve as the very agents and mechanisms for our historical amnesia'.[9] Yet to speak thus disparagingly of media presentations, while at times it might provoke our agreement, seems to me also too simple: the media are not as single in either function or intention as that: Jameson allows for no oppositional voices working in the media, and assumes that the form of this culture cannot produce its own narratives. But perhaps it produces more local, more microcosmic narratives. And ideology is always a matter for contestation; even in the media, it is not static: the media do not always tell the same story as each other for example. The point cannot be settled quite so easily.

A Possible Conclusion

Let me finish with a return to the image of narrative as seduction. If we take seduction as a metaphor, rather than only in its literal, sexual sense, do any of the texts we have thought of or worked from strike you as exemplifying seduction?

I feel that 'The Garden of Forking Paths' does, though neither Richard Madden (his surname is very suggestive) nor the police are likely to be seduced by anything Yu or Albert could say. On the basis of what I have said about the seduction scene in *Anna Karenina*, I think Tolstoy is anxious that the reader should certainly not be seduced by anything of the transgressive. But let me take two examples of where figures in the text do seem to 'seduce' each other. In the Chaucer extract, I am not sure whether the writer is seducing his audience out of their attitudes to monks, or whether the monk is seducing Chaucer the narrator out of his views. Clearly, there is much rhetorical persuasion going on there that might win anyone over. My other example is Wordsworth's 'There was a Boy'. In a way, the boy is trying to seduce the owls by provoking them into a reply, but then the owls and then the rest of nature seduce the boy. In both the Chaucer and the

Wordsworth, seduction seems to me very positive. It implies a two-way process, where we are not sure who is seducing whom. There is no straightforward interpellation. Power is not being exercised in one way only. And that is suggestive that narrative might be very important – and that exposure to narrative might not necessarily be mere submission to ideology. Cannot readings of a text that look not only at its strengths of statement but also at its omissions, its significant gaps, undo that narrative's absolute power, and so prove liberating?

9. Instead of a Conclusion

Every morning brings us news of the globe, and yet we are poor in noteworthy stories. This is because no event any longer comes to us without already being shot through with explanation. In other words, by now almost nothing that happens benefits storytelling; almost everything befits information. Actually, it is half the art of storytelling to keep a story free from explanation as one reproduces it.

(Walter Benjamin: 'The Storyteller')

Narrative seems not only to affect all our thinking, but to be a mode of thinking, the only way it is possible to think. If narrative is so closely tied to ideology, it suggests that how we narrativize – in other words, the very structure of our thinking – is ideological itself. This seems to me an important part of what this *Guide* has argued.

But is there more to be said about the way everyday life is bombarded by different narratives? The sociologist Jean Baudrillard argues that the mark of postmodernism, which is the current situation of most of the western world, is its domination not by tangible forces and controls, but by the messages carried by the media and through the signs that run through society, enabling it to signify its own values to itself. For Baudrillard, these narratives can explain nothing, they do not relate to anything outside of themselves, like real events, for even real events only exist as codified, as packaged in the sign-system of society. Narratives refer only to each other, and there is, for example, no difference discernible in the way an evening's television presents, in virtually identical terms, a comedy show, a drama, the news, sport and a current affairs programme. Each of these forms of narrative is treated in terms of the other, and each only makes sense because of its existence in the same world as the other forms. For Baudrillard it is not just a matter of metanarratives having lost their ability to persuade, as Lyotard argued; rather, there is no possibility of finding a narrative that will stand outside this crazy interchange of narrative signals, where people's lives are narrativized on precisely the same terms as a television programme. People look at images (say on a television soap or on advertising) and form their lives on that basis, while the television forms its own images on the basis of looking at the people. In this swapping of narrative signals, we have the complete triumph of narratives that explain nothing, and the loss of any truth content in the narrative.[1]

If Baudrillard is right and narratives do no more than circulate around each other, including the narratives of our own lives, postmodernism has declared a virtual end to rational statement and narrative that purports to explain. This is what we called a *crisis of representation*: a sense that twentieth-century narratives do not fit, do not refer to existent reality, which is itself not representable. The German Marxist critic Walter Benjamin (1892–1940) reflects in his essay 'The Storyteller' (1936) on the loss of communicable experience evident in the loss of communal, oral storytelling. 'Was it not noticeable at the end of the [First World] war that men returned from the battlefield grown silent – not richer, but poorer in communicable experience?'[2] Perhaps that war was the first to defy the power of possible representations of it.

Benjamin argues that the story-teller has lost ground. First through the advent of the novel, which made experience individual, since most novels are read silently and alone; and so specific that the experience could not be generalized from, but which then went on to explain that experience so fully. Secondly, through the supersession of the novel by newspaper-type 'information' which produces a society with a high valuation placed on instant explanation. What cannot be explained, indeed, ceases to be narratable: think of the need for instant comment that marks out all media presentation of news. For Benjamin:

> the value of information does not survive the moment in which it was new. It lives only at that moment; it has to surrender to it completely and explain itself to it without losing any time. A story is different. It does not expend itself. It preserves and concentrates its strength and is capable of releasing it even after a long time.
>
> (p. 90)

Baudrillard sees explanations as no more than a further circulation of narratives within the total sign-system that makes up our reality. Even if we reject the totalizing effect of his thesis, it should still create in us a scepticism about the possibility of a meaningful narrative.

Narrative may impose on us the need to think in terms of events happening – definable, discrete, manageable events. The Austrian novelist Robert Musil (1880–1942) in his brilliant *The Man Without Qualities* calls the second half 'Seinesgleichen Geschieht', which translates as 'the like of it now happens', or even as 'history repeats itself'. So much of the unfinished novel could be taken as a meditation on narrative, but one suggestion emerging from this title is that we are stuck in a circularity: events are defined as such by being in a narrative – but without a narrative we could never say anything at all about the nature of our lives. But then, what kind of freedom have we to construct any narrative at all which does not immediately codify the 'event' into something the like of which has happened before, and which, therefore, is already known, already absorbed, and somehow dead?

But also, following Benjamin, we could contend for the power of story-telling: seeing stories as capable of infinite re-accentuation and continued usefulness, insofar as they are not tied down to explanation. For example, in his essay, Benjamin recounts a story by Herodotus and meditates on possible explanations that it could yield, while Herodotus gives none: 'that is why this story from ancient Egypt is still capable after thousands of years of arousing astonishment and thoughtfulness. It resembles the seeds of grain which have lain for centuries in the chambers of the pyramids shut up air-tight and have retained their germinative power to this day' (p. 90). If narrative can thus preserve its life, it will in a measure be free from the commanding power of its own historical ideology. Nonetheless, Benjamin sees comparatively little opportunity for the appearance of such unspecifiable, unspecified, local narratives now.[3]

Some questions you might like to think of in going over the arguments advanced in this book:

1   How does Benjamin's distaste for 'information' fit with the postmodernist rejection of the 'grand narrative' and of the meta-narrative, with its offer to explain? Are these the same? Does the level of explanation offered make for a difference?

2   What reasons has the *Guide* advanced to suggest that narratives might be treated with suspicion?

3   I argued that the detective-story form is the paradigm for Aristotelian narration. If this is true, what ideological implications follow for the way we think of narrative, and the way we think of life?

4   Think of alternative ways in which events or people's lives have been narrativized. (Specific media examples might help.) Do the alternative ways support the view that there is bound to be a dominant narrative account, and competing marginal, 'alternative' accounts? How could things be otherwise?

Notes

Place of publication is London, unless otherwise stated. After the first citation, page numbers are given in the text.

Chapter 1

1   Roland Barthes, 'Introduction to the Structural Analysis of Narratives', *Image–Music–Text*, trans. Stephen Heath (Fontana, 1977) p. 79.
2   Michel de Certeau, *The Practice of Everyday Life* (Berkeley: University of California Press, 1984) p. 84.
3   E.M. Forster, *Aspects of the Novel* (1927) (Harmondsworth: Penguin 1963) pp. 33–4.
4   Virginia Woolf, *A Room of One's Own* (Granada, 1977) pp. 70–1; 'Modern Fiction' (1919) in *The Common Reader* (2 vols, Hogarth Press, 1984), vol. 1, p. 150.
5   'Fanny and Annie' (1919) was published with other short stories, in *England, My England* in 1922. Page numbers for the Penguin edition of this (1977 reprint) follow references to *The Penguin Book of English Short Stories*, ed. Christopher Dolley (1967).

Chapter 2

1   In Aristotle, Horace, Longinus, *Classical Literary Criticism*, trans. T.S. Dorsch (Harmondsworth: Penguin) p. 38.
2   F.R. Leavis, *D.H. Lawrence: Novelist* (1955) (Harmondsworth: Penguin, 1964). Leavis's view of narrative is more complex than my use of him suggests. He is strongly anti-Aristotelian in his view of plot, and often dismisses the narrative as of no relevance (e.g. with his readings of *Adam Bede* or *Dombey and Son*) in favour of discovering a textual experience – regarding the demand for plot-line as a rationalization: an abstraction away from the importance of the 'living' moment in the text.
3   Robert Young, *Untying the Text* (Routledge and Kegan Paul, 1981) pp. 155, 156.
4   Roland Barthes, *S/Z* (1970); trans. Richard Howard (New York: Hill and Wang, 1974) p. 204.
5   I discuss 'literariness' in *What is Literary Language?* ch. 4. Jakobson proposes that attention to utterance offered as literature should focus on what is 'poetic' in it; meaning not that which is traditionally

'literary', but that which calls attention to itself, rather than to the content of the message. This self-consciousness of utterance draws attention to the level of the *signifier*, not the *signified*, and works away from mere easily understood referential meaning – indeed, 'defamiliarizes' it.

6 On ideology, a useful beginning can be made from the entry in Raymond Williams, *Keywords* (Fontana, 1976) and his *Marxism and Literature* (Oxford: OUP, 1977) ch. 4 and section II generally. Williams sees ideology as inseparably connected to 'culture' – both the whole lived practices of a society, and the productions of that society: see for instance his *Culture* (Fontana, 1981) pp. 26–30. What a society produces may function as part of its ideology, but the text also stands in a complex relationship to the dominant ideology.

Chapter 3

1 Gerard Genette, *Narrative Discourse Revisited* (1983); trans. Jane E. Lewin (New York: Cornell U.P., 1988) p. 13. I quote also from Genette, *Narrative Discourse: An essay in method* (1972); trans. Jane E. Lewin (New York: Cornell U.P., 1980), and from *Figures of Literary Discourse*, trans. Alan Sheridan (Oxford: Blackwell, 1982). A good starting essay by Genette appears in J. Hillis Miller (ed.) *Aspects of Narrative* (New York: Columbia U.P., 1971).

   Some key texts of 'narratology': *Morphology of the Folktale* (2nd. edn) (Austin: Texas U.P., 1968); Mieke Bal, *Narratology: Introduction to the Theory of Narrative* (1980); trans. Christine van Boheemen (Toronto U.P., 1985); Gerald Prince, *The Form and Functioning of Narrative* (Berlin: Mouton, 1982), and the work of Claude Bremond (*Logique du Récit*, Paris: Seuil, 1973) and A.J. Greimas. Articles by both are available in English: e.g. Bremond's 'Morphology of the French Folktale', *Semiotica* 2 (1969) 247–76. *New Literary History* 20 (Spring 1989) is devoted to Greimas's work.

2 The issue of tense, which I say no more about in this *Guide*, applies more to French literary texts where 'classical' French writing – roughly that between 1650 and 1850 – used the aorist tense, which promotes the sense of clear, definable events, playing down the role of the narrator, and thus making the events seem natural, not artificially produced as the effect of ideology. Flaubert broke with this usage, and issues of which tense is used have been important since.

3 Plato held all art to be diegetic, in that it told a story, but took mimesis (i.e. dramatic art) to be an aspect of diegesis. Aristotle in contrast took diegesis as an aspect of mimesis, but actually he did not hold all art to be mimetic, though he wished it to be so: in epic, where poets speak in their own person, 'little of what they write is impersonal representation' (*Poetics*, ch. 24, p. 68).

   On the basis of chs 3 and 4, the mimesis/diegesis distinction may not be very useful, since the narrator is also a dramatic fiction: all is representation. The narrator (even if s/he is called the author) is another dramatic voice. Yet, to follow Gerard Genette in *Figures of*

Literary Discourse, no literature is mimetic in the sense that Plato and Aristotle considered it: i.e. in drama and dramatic speech. All rendering of speech is artifice; even the language of soap operas is highly conventionalized (with deleted expletives, characters talking in sentences, and talking in a way which carries forward a narrative). The conversations you hold at your breakfast table could never be transferred neat to a soap opera script: the script has to be artificial in order to look real. In a novel, the only bits which would be mimetic (imitating reality) would be 'he said' and 'she replied'. But those are precisely what Plato saw as diegesis and an imperfect imitation of reality.

Narrative, which Genette defines as 'the representation of an event or a sequence of events, real or fictitious, by means of language, and more particularly by means of written language' (p. 127) is thus the mode of discourse that knows there can be nothing but conventional representation – i.e. diegesis; that mimesis is diegesis. Art cannot mirror the real world or describe it as it is. Indeed, at moments Aristotle recognized this, saying that in literature 'there are not the same standards of correctness as in political theory' (*Poetics*, ch. 25, p. 69). This suggests that art is not bound to follow literal truth; and that when it goes its own way the result is not falsehood, as Plato would have said, but fiction.

4 Louis Althusser, 'Ideology and Ideological State Apparatuses', *Lenin and Philosophy*, trans. Ben Brewster (New Left Books, 1971) p. 153. It is possible to separate Althusser's sense of interpellation from some of the more contentious arguments about ideology he raises: that Marxism in its explanatory power may be considered a science outside ideology, for instance. The power of ideology to secure people's assent to the ruling classes Althusser derives from Gramsci. Ted Benton, *The Rise and Fall of Structural Marxism* (Macmillan, 1984) is useful as a critique of Althusser; *Diacritics* 20 (Winter 1985) gives its whole issue to a consideration of post-Althusserian Marxism. The reader *Culture, Ideology and Social Process*, ed. Tony Bennett *et al.* (Batsford and Open University Press, 1981) gathers several relevant texts on ideology.

5 The translation here, which does not smooth out the difficulties the text poses, and is sensitive to its hints and ambiguities, is by my colleague Jonathan Hall, to whom I am very grateful. Other translations appear in Jorge Luis Borges, *Dreamtigers* (1964); trans. Mildred Boyer (Souvenir Press, 1971), p. 51, and in *Labyrinths* (Harmondsworth: Penguin, 1981), pp. 282–3.

6 Emile Benveniste, *Problems in General Linguistics* (1966); trans. Mary Elizabeth Meek (Florida: Miami U.P., 1971). See chs 20, 21.

> I use 'I' only when I am speaking to someone who will be a *you* in my address. It is this condition of dialogue that is constitutive of person, for it implies that reciprocally, *I* becomes *you* in the address of the one who in his turn designates himself as I. . . . Language is possible only because each speaker sets himself up as a *subject* by referring to himself as *I* in his discourse. (pp. 224–5)

On p. 226, Beneveniste uses 'deixis' (a referent determined only by a relation to the speaker), taking the term from Jakobson, *Selected Writings*, vol. 2 (The Hague: Mouton), pp. 130–47.

Chapter 4

1   Michel Foucault, 'What is an Author?' *Language: Counter-Memory, Practice* (New York, Cornell U.P., 1977) p. 138.

2   Colin MacCabe, *Popular Television and Film*, ed. Tony Bennett *et al.* (BFI and Open University Press, 1981) p. 217. See also the course reader, Michael Gurevitch, Tony Bennett, James Curran and Janet Woollacott (eds), *Culture, Society and the Media* (Methuen, 1982). For the work on *A Christmas Carol*, I have drawn on F.W. Stanzel, *A Theory of Narrative* (1982); trans. Charlotte Goedsche (Cambridge: CUP, 1984), a study which sets itself in contrast to Genette, but makes much more of the narrator.

3   For free indirect discourse, see Roy Pascal, *The Dual Voice* (Manchester: Manchester U.P., 1977).

4   Percy Lubbock, *The Craft of Fiction* (1921) (New York: Viking Press reprint, 1957).

5   James Joyce, *A Portrait of the Artist as a Young Man* (Harmondsworth: Penguin, 1960) p. 215; T.S. Eliot, *Selected Essays* (Faber, 1951) p. 17.

6   One important attempt to rehabilitate the author appears in Wayne C. Booth, *The Rhetoric of Fiction* (Chicago: Chicago U.P., 1961), who tried rescuing the author and the author's right to 'tell' from Lubbock's insistence on 'showing'. Booth's aim is to show that the author is not so quickly eliminated as the central and final arbiter; he wants to 'pursue the author's means of controlling his reader' (Preface). The right to 'tell' produces a text in which the implied author appears: the writer creates an implied version of himself, discovering himself as he writes: producing a second self through the text, with 'various commitments, secret or overt' (p. 71). Each text produces its own implied author. Thus each implied author is actually an effect of the rhetorical stratagems of the text, improvised for the moment, not of the author him/herself.

    If we keep the concept of the implied author, it would be with the reservation that the reader's projection of what kind of person wrote the text – what kind of author could have written this way – is itself ideological. Think of how different periods have imagined Shakespeare, for example, all in ways which relate to the particular dominant ideology.

7   In contrast to Genette's sense of the narrator and where s/he stands is Bakhtin (discussed in *What is Literary Language*, pp. 31–5) all of whose work attempts to show the dialogic, double, non-single centred nature of narrative. Bakhtin argues that all utterance is marked out by the presence of the other (this fits with 'Borges and I'). Speech reveals the impossibility of singleness, of an isolated subjectivity. Bakhtin's sense of the polyphonic nature of discourse

has sometimes been confused with indirect free speech. But that is a technique by which the text resists the attempt to make a certain statement clearly attributable. Bakhtin, in contrast, deals with something that is not a technique, but an aspect of writing itself: arguing that any utterance resists classification as one voice or another's: it is inevitably plural.

Chapter 5

1 On Aristotle, I refer to Humphry House, *Aristotle's Poetics*, ed. Colin Hardie (Hart Davis, 1956); Elder Olson (ed.) *Aristotle's Poetics and English Literature* (Chicago: Chicago U.P., 1965); Stephen Halliwell, *Aristotle's Poetics* (Duckworth, 1986) p. 151. For an influential application of Aristotle, see R.S. Crane, *Critics and Criticism: Ancient and Modern* (Chicago: Chicago U.P., 1952).

2 Matthew Arnold, *Essays in Criticism* (Everyman, 1964) p. 354.

3 'Closure' in this sense comes from Barbara Heinstein Smith, *Poetic Closure: A Study of how Poems End* (Chicago: Chicago U.P., 1968). See also Frank Kermode, *The Sense of an Ending* (Oxford: OUP, 1967). The theme is pursued in Marianne Torgovnick, *Closure in the Novel* (Princeton, 1981). Each of these studies uses the Aristotelian conception of plot. *Nineteenth Century Fiction* 33 (1978) gives a whole issue to the problem of narrative endings.

4 Sophocles, *The Theban Plays*, trans. E.F. Watling (Harmondsworth: Penguin, 1947) p. 37.

5 Jessie Chambers [E.T.], *D.H. Lawrence: A Personal Record* (Cambridge: CUP, 1980) p. 105.

6 This discussion of the mirror depends on Jacques Lacan's psychoanalytic work on the formation of a primary narcissism through the child's early identification with its image in the mirror: this Imaginary phase, 'the mirror phase' remains a possibility which narrative encourages with its invitations to identifications (see below, ch. 6). Lacan, *Ecrits: A Selection*, trans. Alan Sheridan (Tavistock Publications, 1977) pp. 1–9. Lacan argues that the child has to learn a new, subject position in the 'symbolic' order, which comes into play with language-learning, and with the recognition of the power of patriarchy.

7 Michel Foucault discusses the constitution of the subject in *The History of Sexuality* (Harmondsworth: Penguin, 1984) p. 60.

8 Again, the work of Mikhail Bakhtin is relevant here: see *The Dialogic Imagination* (Austin: Texas University Press, 1981). See above, ch. 4 note 7.

9 I discuss the implications of J.L. Austin's sense of the performative (= rhetorical, persuasive, rather than simply stating) in *What is Literary Language*, p. 56.

10 Jill Mann, *Chaucer and Medieval Narrative* (Cambridge: CUP, 1972) pp. 36–7.

11 Paul de Man, *The Rhetoric of Romanticism* (New York: Columbia University Press, 1984) p. 73.

Chapter 6

1   Roland Barthes, *Mythologies* (1957); trans. Annette Lavers (Paladin, 1973) p. 129.

2   Laura Mulvey, *Visual and Other Pleasures* (Macmillan, 1989). See also Teresa de Lauretis, *Alice Doesn't* (Bloomington: Indiana U.P., 1984) taking up Mulvey's ground: ch. 5 'Desire in Narrative' is relevant.

3   Roland Barthes, *The Pleasure of the Text* (1973) (Oxford: Blackwell, 1990) pp. 47, 10. I can only refer here to the objections that some feminist writers raise to the masculinist cast of these arguments about the Oedipal; the work of Lacan has provided one point of intervention here. See Juliet Mitchell and Jacqueline Rose, *Feminine Sexuality* (Macmillan, 1982); on the narratives unmotivated by the Oedipal competitive, the work of Virginia Woolf (e.g. *A Room of One's Own*) is crucial; much feminist writing begins from there. Gilles Deleuze and Felix Guattari see the Oedipal as an aspect of ideology: on this, see Elizabeth Wright, *Psychoanalytic Criticism* (Methuen, 1984) ch. 9, 'Psychoanalysis and Ideology'. For the family as the source of the 'double bind' which both creates and frustrates narrative, see Bill Nichols' use of Gregory Bateson's work in discussion of film texts, such as the narrative of Hitchcock's film *The Birds* in his *Ideology and the Image* (Bloomington, Indiana U.P., 1981) pp. 98–103, 133–69.

4   Apart from 'Beyond the Pleasure Principle' itself, see on the issues here Peter Brooks, *Reading for the Plot* (Oxford: Clarendon, 1984), which discusses the temporal dynamics involved in reading (pressing on to the end: an argument of 'Beyond the Pleasure Principle', which Brooks reads as Freud's 'master-plot'). Narratology, Brooks argues, neglects this onward dynamic. Brooks's study is important, but I have two reservations about it. He reads Freud's essay as though it had a determinate argument and an objectivity: with this compare Derrida's argument about it as speculation in *The Post-card: From Socrates to Freud*. Secondly, he takes an Aristotelian view of plot, seeing the ending as binding: thus 'narrative always makes the implicit claim to be in a state of repetition, as a going over again of a ground already covered: a *sjuzet* repeating the *fabula*, as the detective retraces the tracks of the criminal' (p. 97). This works for some narratives (e.g. confessions), but it presents a positivistic view of narrative in itself.

5   D.A. Miller, *Narrative and its Discontents* (Princeton, 1981) p. ix.

Chapter 7

1   Jorge Luis Borges, *Labyrinths* (Harmondsworth: Penguin, 1970) pp. 44–54. Page references are given in brackets.

2   Christian Metz, *Film Language* (New York: Oxford University Press, 1974) p. 18.

3   Terry Eagleton, *Criticism and Ideology* (New Left Books, 1976) p. 77. This question of the relationship of the text to ideology deserves more space than I can give it, but Pam Morris in her reading of